INTIMATE FEEDBACK

A lovers' guide to
getting in touch with each other

*Barrie Hopson and
Charlotte Hopson*

SIMON AND SCHUSTER · NEW YORK

DESIGNED BY EVE METZ

MANUFACTURED IN THE UNITED STATES OF AMERICA

1 2 3 4 5 6 7 8 9 10

Library of Congress Cataloging in Publication Data
Hopson, Barrie.
    Intimate feedback.

    First published in 1973 under title: Twosome plus.
    Bibliography: p. 221
    1. Marriage.   2. Interpersonal relations.   3. Intimacy (Psy-
chology)   I. Hopson, Charlotte, joint author.   II. Title.
HQ734.H82   1974   301.42'7   74–9860
ISBN 0–671–21793–3

To Caitlin and Barnaby
live every breath of your being
experience each call from your
senses,
seek out that which you can love
in each person,
and above all be honest with
yourself about yourself—and
you will grow.

ACKNOWLEDGMENTS

The stimulus to write this book came from Peter Farrell, who walked into my office trying to sell me academic textbooks and instead persuaded me to write a book. He then persuaded Charlotte to write it with me, and thus we began.

Innocents abroad in the world of commercial publishing, we turned endlessly to Diana Crawfurd for help with the technicalities of actually getting the book into a publishable form—help which entailed a good deal of generosity and patience on her part.

The many couples we talked to had the greatest influence on our ideas. Without them there would have been no book at all.

My own interest in the human potential movement, which resulted in the exercises contained in the book, was nurtured by our close relationship with John and Sarah Adams.

Without Barbara Haig to bravely look after our children on occasions, and Pamela Green, who did most of the secretarial and typing work, we would still be working.

Barrie Hopson

Contents

my feet begin to tap" conflicts . . . manufactured conflicts . . . transparent conflicts . . . solving problems together . . . how to generate change . . . masterminding . . . making decisions together . . . to make a decision or to avoid it? . . . proactive decision making . . . proactive decision avoidance.

beware the double bind . . . more verbal traps . . . nonverbal communication.

man cannot marry for bread alone . . . are you old enough for marriage? . . . how important are engagements? . . . to bed or not to bed? . . . do children help a marriage? . . . like father, like son . . . does social class matter? . . . are some people better suited to marriage? . . . myths about marriage . . . mate selection and marital success . . . twogetherness or togetherness?

marriage—public health problem no. 1 . . . the functions of marriage . . . marriages of convenience . . . intimate marriage . . . alternatives to legal marriage . . . the exploding marriage—destruction or recreation?

Introduction

Text	Subtext
Text	*Subtext*
What is said	What is meant
PATRICIA:	
"God, it's so boring here all day . . . the predictability of washing diapers, feeding children, changing diapers, washing dishes, preparing *your* meal . . ."	He cannot possibly understand the drudgery and sameness of my days. Why should it automatically be me, rather than him, who ends up doing this soul-destroying work?
JOHN:	
"I realize it must be boring for you, but I try to help as much as I can."	You don't appreciate the sacrifices I am making in my career just because you can't cope with two children like other women seem to manage to do.
PATRICIA:	
"Well, it's not enough. You wouldn't do this job. You're out all hours. I could just about manage if you were around here some of the time."	You might think that you are here and help out but, compared to the time that I spend with these children, you do nothing.

JOHN:

"Well, I do have to go to work sometimes, you know. I am given a salary for which I'm expected to do something."

You wouldn't be so happy if I didn't earn enough money to provide you with your own car, washing machine, dishwasher and a big house, with no money problems. Yet somehow you expect to have all this without me doing anything. You're just damned unreasonable.

PATRICIA:

"I don't blame you. I wouldn't want to come back to this dump—with a nagging wife and screaming kids."

I do blame you and this whole damned society for making it so unfair for women. I also feel guilty that I do make so many demands.

JOHN:

"Oh, let's not have that routine. You're just never satisfied, no matter what I do. I'm slipping behind in my work as it is."

You don't realize what I am sacrificing for you, you selfish bitch.

PATRICIA:

"Oh, so now you're going to try to make me feel guilty for forcing you away from work. Well, if you don't want to be here for your own sake, I don't want you to be here for mine."

I hate you for always making me feel inadequate.

JOHN:

"But I *do* want to be here. I like being at home, but you just don't appreciate it. I'm home with you much more than most men are with their wives." Of course I wouldn't be here so much if you didn't make me feel so goddam guilty. You don't seem to realize what a saint you've got in me.

PATRICIA:

"That does it. I hardly ever see you. You come home, pick up the kids and play with them like little dolls and you put them down when you've been entertained enough. You get all the gravy. On weekends it's the same, while you're relaxing reading papers I'm doing the same work as I have to do every other day of the week." You think you're so generous. I wish you had my life for a week. You would see what it is like: God, I hate you for making me feel like such a bitch.

This is not an unfamiliar kind of row between a husband and a wife. The content changes from couple to couple and from time to time, but the form is depressingly familiar. Why is it depressing? Not because they are fighting—that shows that there is vitality in the relationship. It is depressing because they are on a merry-go-round that will only make them giddy. They do not know how to get off and, in the process, are making themselves sick with one another and with themselves.

This book is about relationships. It assumes that intimate relationships, whether between men and women, men and men, or women and women, are essential if people wish their lives to be meaningful. It is concerned with personal growth, attained not by being a "loner," self-reliant and sitting on one's own mountain peak, but through relationships. Relationships can be a cage which prevents you from discovering the world and yourself, or they can be as a home, providing a secure base from which to explore the outside world and providing significance for your own being.

Take two helpings of understanding, more than a few grains of tolerance and leave to simmer for forty years.

Many books on marriage give rise to the expectation that a choice recipe for marital bliss is contained within their covers. The only problem with recipes is that some people thrive on them, but for others they sound too much like hard work. The world of cookery has recently been flooded with recipe books for the "bad cook," the "lazy cook," the "instant cook." Our book is not for the "bad" husband or the "lazy" wife, but simply for the average couple who retain some interest in their relationship.

This will, for most people, mean a legally defined marital relationship. For even today, with more divorce cases, unmarried people living together, homosexual relationships and commune experiments, well over 90 percent of the population marry at some time in their lives, and the nuclear family is by far the dominant living pattern. However, all of the exercises and everything we have to say about "marriage" apply to any long-term relationship between two people who live together and are emotionally committed to one another.

Observing a marriage—whether it is your own or someone else's—is rather like looking through a kaleidoscope. The pattern constantly changes, new colors are born, old forms die away. Perhaps one is not always certain just who twists the kaleidoscope, but that can add to the magic.

One reason for writing this book was a fascination we shared in watching new marital patterns emerge in our society. Some people feel that marriage has disintegrated and that this is either a very good or depressingly bad thing. Certainly more and more families are experiencing nuclear explosions, the pollution level being carefully recorded by the divorce courts. But what excites us are the entirely new forms of marriage with which people are experimenting, along with the less dramatic but no less significant innovations which individual couples are introducing to the well-worn clichés of marital living.

We have been appalled at the amount of gray, fifth-best mediocrity that people from all walks of life are prepared to put up with in their relationships. There must be more genuinely lonely people in marriage than outside it.

As a result of our experiences within our own marriage and numerous case studies and interviews with people about their marriages, we decided to collect some exercises together that might help others to get their marriages moving again. Most of these exercises have been developed for this book, some are borrowed, some half-remembered from the archives of the collective unconscious that trainers of group dynamics and personal growth workshops carry around with them. The exercises are appropriate for couples who have been married for years, for those just contemplating matrimony and for those who simply want to explore a deep, personal relationship with another human being.

The greatest danger in writing a book of this kind is that marriage can be made to sound about as exciting as an underdone suet pudding. Perhaps this is why so many behavioral scientists have scurried away from analyzing experiences like love, hate, ecstasy and despair. The scientist, by the very nature of his trade, reduces them to the banal, while the poet, by virtue of his art, breathes life into them.

The psychologist Sidney Jourard puts it like this:

I defined love as freely expressed behaviour, undertaken with the aim of fostering happiness and growth in the person loved. But there is something grim and joyless in that conception of love. I would like to spice this conception with some laughter, some wholesome, lusty, fully expressed, mischievous, lecherous, saucy sex. Not sex as mere coupling, but sex as an experience of *joie de vivre,* of sharing of the good things in life.

A good book about marriage should have an ample sprinkling of blood, sweat, semen and tears on well-thumbed pages. We hope that this book does not look too neat on your shelf when you have finished with it. For neat and tidy books, like neat and tidy lives, have not been lived in.

Barrie Hopson and Charlotte Hopson

If I had only . . .
forgotten future greatness
and looked at the green things and the buildings
and reached out to those around me
and smelled the air
and ignored the forms and the self-styled obligations
and heard the rain on the roof
and put my arms around my wife
. . . and it's not too late

HUGH PRATHER

now is the only time
to take the wafer of our sacrament
before it vanishes.
This is all there is.

PETER GOBLIN

1·The Out-of-Touch Society

We apologize for contributing yet another "society" to the annals of sensationalist sociology. We have had the acquisitive society, the affluent society, the great society, the bureaucratic society, the transient society, the anxious society, the achieving society, the unprepared society, and the mass society closely pursued by the mass communication society. The danger of eye-catching titles is that the grain of truth contained in the argument is lost amid a welter of generalizations that diffuses the grain over such an acreage of paper that it is lost in the authors' need to produce a book from an insight. Instead of writing a book about a society, we have written a chapter because, to understand the complexities of modern marriage, it is necessary to look at the social context in which it lives and breathes.

The central point is that we live in a society where people are finding it increasingly difficult to relate to one another and consequently to themselves. Many people are not only *figuratively* "out of touch" with others and themselves but *literally* "out of touch" also. In an intellectually oriented society too many people have mislaid their sensuality.

The most popular artistic contributions of this era, on stage, in literature and in art, have been those which have expressed feelings of alienation, apathy and nihilism. The hero of the postwar era has been the "outsider," popularized in the 1950s by Colin Wilson, who crystallized the feelings of a generation. The antiheroes of *Room at the Top* and *Satur-*

day Night and Sunday Morning were resigned to what they perceived to be the inevitable lack of meaning in life, whether in the boardroom, the bedroom or on the shop floor. In America the "beat generation," disgusted with the external world in which they found themselves, embarked on a journey into the interior of their souls via the Far East, Kerouac, hallucinogenic drugs, Timothy Leary, and encounter groups. This "trip" took a decade and still continues. Existentialist philosophers write like poets but are more widely read; poets write like existentialist philosophers on an acid trip.

It is not our purpose to provide a chronological account of events that have produced the problems of modern living. Suffice it to make a few general comments.

ALIENATION

Men are becoming increasingly alienated from other men and from themselves.

Beginning with school, if not before, an individual is systematically stripped of his imagination, his creativity, his heritage, his dreams and his personal uniqueness, in order to style him into a productive unit for a mass technological society. Instinct, feeling and spontaneity are repressed by overwhelming forces. As the individual is drawn into the meritocracy, his working life is split from his home life, and both suffer from a lack of wholeness. Eventually, people virtually become their professions, roles or occupations, and are thenceforth strangers to themselves.

Charles Reich[1]

Because we live restricted lives in unsatisfying jobs, yet are too tired or bored to profit from State-provided leisure, we live a life rich in ritual, routine and habit. In the process, we

1. *The Greening of America,* Random House, New York, 1970.

have often lost touch with our feelings, lost confidence in our ability to act and innovate and lost the capacity for joy, sensuality and creativity. We are seduced by material goodies, we earn more and more money to provide us with greater freedom to have what we want, only to learn what William James told us eighty years ago, that "lives based on having are less free than lives based either on doing or on being."

The irony is that it is in an age of intensive and extensive communication that so many people report their inability to tune in to themselves.

Some of the most significant dramatists of our time take as their subject matter the breakdown of interpersonal communication. Ionesco, Beckett and Pinter picture situations where people glide past each other like ships in the night, rarely touching, engaged in a monologue with themselves.

ALIENATION BREEDS VIOLENCE

The mood of the anonymous person is, if I cannot affect or touch anybody, I can at least shock you into some feeling, force you into some passion through wounds and pain; I shall at least make sure we both feel something, and I shall force you to see me and know that I also am here!

Rollo May[2]

These sentiments are only too familiar to the marriage counselor or student of marriage.

LACK OF COMMITMENTS

Rollo May's central point is that we have forgotten how to love and, just as important, how to "will." By this, he means

2. *Love and Will*, W. W. Norton, New York, 1969.

how to make an impact on a malleable world. We are hypnotized by our feelings of powerlessness and use this as an excuse for doing nothing.

. . . the central core of modern man's "neurosis," it may be fairly said, is the undermining of his experience of himself as responsible, the sapping of his will and ability to make decisions. The lack of will is much more than merely an ethical problem: the modern individual so often has the conviction that even if he did exert his "will"—or whatever illusion passes for it—his actions wouldn't do any good anyway. It is this inner experience of impotence, this contradiction in will, which constitutes our critical problem.

Rollo May[3]

The social sciences, with their deterministic orientation, have provided us with too many excuses about why we are in such an unhappy job, marriage or mood.

Man is distinguished by his capacity to know that he is determined, and to choose his relationship to what determines him. He can and must, unless he abdicates his consciousness, choose how he will relate to necessity, such as death, old age, limitations of intelligence, and the conditioning inescapable in his own background. Will he accept this necessity, deny it, fight it, affirm it, consent to it?

Rollo May[4]

May claims that we are "co-creators of our fate." Yet we live in an age where people constantly bemoan, "We can do noth-

3. *Ibid.*
4. *Ibid.*

ing, we are powerless." It may be difficult to affect a war in Vietnam, major environmental pollution and a host of other things, but one has the power to influence one's own life, and one is responsible for what is done with it. To pretend otherwise is self-deceit.

If you have an unhappy marriage you are largely to blame for it. Either you should be trying to change it, or you should be ending it—presuming, of course, that you really do want a happy marriage.

In Chapter 4 we describe people as primarily *proactive* or *reactive*. That is, you are the sort of person either who makes things happen or who allows things to happen to you. Unfortunately, there is evidence that even in the last decade American college students are more reactive than they were.[5]

The exercises in this book are intended to help generate a proactive approach to your own marriage.

Unfortunately, our educational system does not teach our children how to make decisions—only to abide by decisions others have made on their behalf. The more that people realize that they do have the power to choose what happens to them, the greater becomes the possibility of creating a society of committed people. This is desirable in the sense that commitment signifies that one's existence has a meaning. For far too many people, existence is meaningless and life intolerable. They need to prove to themselves that they do have the ability to force their will upon a malleable world. To do this is an act of creation, and creativity and lack of meaning are totally incompatible bedfellows.

Marriage is an act of commitment. Therein lies its strength and its dangers. Commitments can become ties. The voluntary surrender of certain areas of freedom is all too often translated into a denial of a way of life one would prefer. It

5. Julian Rotter, "External versus Internal Control," *Psychology Today,* June 1971.

is when surrender is converted to sacrifice that a marriage has problems.

THE AGE OF TRANSIENCE

We live in a society where the only constant phenomenon is change, where the only security is in the knowledge that tomorrow is going to be very different from today and that yesterday will be the subject matter for next year's history syllabus. Alvin Toffler in his apocalyptic book *Future Shock*[6] claims that a combination of transience, increasing diversity and novelty in our life styles, organizations and institutions produces the phenomenon of "future shock"—a pathological state which is increasingly afflicting people who cannot cope in an age of "overchoice." Jobs are changed more frequently, homes moved, fashions adopted and discarded, knowledge gained and outdated, ideas created and consumed faster and faster. Not only do possessions and information become increasingly temporary but subcults and life and work patterns, including marriage, become increasingly diverse. Totally new concepts in biology and technology reduce us to the status of naïve visitors watching a world riding an acceleration course toward advances far exceeding anything that man is psychologically or morally prepared to live with in comfort.

The symptoms of the disease called future shock are with us already—anxiety, psychosomatic illnesses, depression, apathy and violence. Its victims often display erratic swings in interest and life style, accompanied by feelings of harassment and stress and a need to escape from the large number of decisions they are ill-equipped to make.

In the United Kingdom a working man can expect 3 or 4 major occupational changes in his working lifetime.

6. Random House, New York, 1970.

In the United States at the beginning of the 1960s the average 20-year-old man could be expected to change jobs 6 or 7 times.

In the USA 25 percent of present-day workers are in occupations that did not exist 25 years ago. It is estimated that by 1990 75 percent of the American population will be in jobs that do not yet exist.

1 in 9 British marriages end in divorce.

1 in 4 American marriages end in divorce.

1 in 9 American children come from homes broken by divorce, death or separation.

In the UK in 1961 11 percent of the population had been in their present residence for less than one year.

The average life of a mortgage in the UK is 8 years.

In the USA 1 in 5 people change their address every year.

At the rate at which knowledge is accumulating, by the time the child born today completes his education the amount of knowledge in the world will be 4 times greater than now. By the time he is 50, it will be 32 times greater, and 97 percent of everything known in the world will have been acquired within his lifetime.

Perhaps one of the most disturbing aspects of transience is its effect on human relationships. Toffler quotes evidence to suggest that we meet more and more people in modern life because of our increased mobility, and this, by implication, means the *average* interpersonal relationship is likely to be shorter in duration. We will have to learn to measure the value of a relationship in terms of its quality rather than its quantity, that is, its length.

The new catch phrase is likely to be "how to *lose* friends and influence people."

Individuals will develop the ability to form loose "buddy-type" relationships on the basis of common interests or subgroup affilia-

tions, and to easily leave these friendships, moving either to an-
other location and joining a similar interest group or to another
interest group within the same location . . . This ability to form
and then to drop, or lower the level of acquaintanceship, close
relationships quickly, coupled with increased mobility, will result
in any given individual forming many more friendships than is
possible for most in the present.

Courtney Tall[7]

Meanwhile, the sales of Christmas cards continue to boom!

The question that remains is whether "temporary marriage" will be, as Toffler maintains, the dominant feature of family life in the future.

BODILY ALIENATION

We are not only out of touch with one another, but also we do not touch one another physically. Before we can be confident of our identity we need to have it affirmed by others. They can do this in two ways: talk to us, or touch us. Berne[8] talks about the human need to be "stroked." This is physical during the first years of life, but then in our society "stroking" becomes increasingly figurative through verbal contact only.

We are encouraged not to be in touch with our own bodies or other people's bodies.[9] Jourard[10] wished to discover how much people were touched by their parents and friends. He found that college students were touched most by their mothers and by friends of the opposite sex. For many of them their fathers touched no more than hands.

In our culture to touch someone is such a blatant demonstration of intimacy that we think very carefully before acting.

7. Quoted in *Future Shock, op. cit.,* p. 97.
8. *Games People Play,* Grove Press, New York, 1964.
9. See p. 110 for an account of intercultural differences in bodily contact.
10. S. M. Jourard, "An Exploratory Study of Body-Accessibility," *British Journal of Social and Clinical Psychology,* 5 (1966), 221–231.

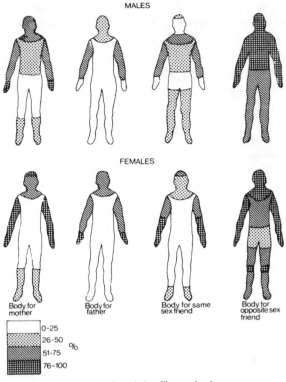

MALES

FEMALES

| Body for mother | Body for father | Body for same sex friend | Body for opposite sex friend |

0-25
26-50 %
51-75
76-100

Areas of the body involved in bodily contact

But because of this an important channel of interpersonal communication is closed. It appears to be difficult enough for many people to communicate verbally with their fellows without creating extra difficulties.

Because we rarely use our bodies in our relationships they remain strange to us. We become cerebral beings with appendages. Yet positive feelings about our own bodies are essential to our mental health. Secord and Jourard[11] found

11. "The Appraisal of Body Cathexis: Body Cathexis and the Self," *Journal of Consulting Psychology,* 17 (1953), 343-347.

that the person who had negative feelings about his body was also likely to feel negatively about himself as a total person.

There is increasing evidence to suggest that it is important to be in touch with our own bodies on grounds of physical health. Psychosomatic medicine has long made a strong case for the fact that emotional states affect the body. But more recently there have been advocates for the opposing view, that bodily states affect the feelings—"somatopsychic."

The man whose predominant set is fear will certainly betray it in the carriage of his head, neck, shoulders and rib cage. His defensive lack of ease will show as physical as well as psychological tension. There may be physiological imbalances of many sorts, e.g., a disturbance of the sympathetic–para-sympathetic nervous balance which must be present for the maintenance of good digestion: tensions and irregularities of the rib cage itself may become apparent as asthma, even as a disturbance of normal cardiac function. A head consistently thrust forward gives rise to an anterior displacement of the neck which will not be accessible to voluntary correction, nor to the directive: "Get your head up!" The resulting symptoms may vary from repetitive headaches to a shoulder bursitis. Various functions too, can be affected through restriction of the vagus nerve.

Ida Rolf[12]

The human potential movement has placed great emphasis on the task of getting in touch and gaining control of one's body.

GETTING-IN-TOUCH MOVEMENTS

This combination of alienation, lack of commitment and fear of physical intimacy in an age of instability makes people

12. "Structured Integration," *Systematics*, 1 No. 1 (1963).

afraid of their own humanity. Perhaps it might let us down, so we are exhorted on all sides to

Keep contacts minimal or at least shallow.
Don't really look at the other (or at least don't see him).
Never touch—unless for sex, to hurt, or to control.
Avoid listening, certainly do not hear.

Rollo May

We have entered a psychological ice age. Except for occasional bursts of warmth, often fueled by sex after a few cocktails, truly intimate encounter has begun to disappear from civilized Western life.

George Bach and Peter Wyden[13]

As a reaction to this, the human potential movement has been developing in the United States over the past decade, and the first shock waves have already been felt in England. The range of *titles* for such movements is widespread—sensitivity groups, encounter groups, "touchie-feelies," marathon weekends, gestalt workshops, bio-energetic sessions, sensory awareness, nude encounter, search for joy. There is much that is easy to make fun of. The mass media have had a heyday from films like *Bob and Carol, Ted and Alice,* to seemingly endless magazine articles and television documentaries. But, in spite of the excesses and commercialism of some of these movements, there is an Ideal of Man which radiates through the dollar curtains—the feeling, caring, generous, spontaneous, authentic man.

The goals of the getting-in-touch movements include: to search for a genuine personal identity; to sense and feel the difference and sameness between ourselves and our world; to

13. *The Intimate Enemy,* Morrow, New York, 1969.

achieve interpersonal understanding through accepting the feelings of ourselves and others; to break down the codes of interpersonal ritual and hypocrisy; to establish the confidence to live through our bodies as well as our heads; to eliminate intellectual defensiveness as a barrier to insights into the nature of our being; to tune in to emotional and sensual wavelengths previously jammed only too effectively by socialization; to develop commitments to ourselves and to others; to be warm, compassionate, but honest.

The danger of the movement is that at present it remains a middle-class recreation. "Let us be warm, feeling people— on weekends, for on Monday it's back to Robotville." But they all do go back!

It gives its participants a sense of being liberated, enlightened, and sophisticated, in tune with the advanced themes of the day and the movements of the young, and to that extent gives them a sense of renewed youth and freshness—a brief diet of uninhibitedness that doubtless middle-class life sorely needs. But the issue still remains whether this is any more than peronal release or indulgent recreation with a façade of sophisticated "advanced" ideology or myth to give it sanction and respectability.

Bernard G. Rosenthal[14]

One sympathetic observer has called some encounter weekends "nothing more than expensive bawdy houses with a serving-up of intellectual dessert." There are undoubtedly middle-class "groupies" who flit from guru to guru, from one new experience to another, like peak-experience-seeking Don Juans.

14. "The Nature and Development of the Encounter Group Movement," *Confrontation: Encounters in Self and Interpersonal Awareness,* ed. L. Blank, G. Gottsegen, M. Gottsegen, Macmillan, New York, 1971.

I have met (or better, not encountered) numerous people whom I think of as "T-group bums," or encounter-group bloodhounds —who can enter a town . . ., sniff the air, and say, "There's an encounter group going on somewhere," and they track it down. Once in, they cry, swear, touch, and insist people stop the bullshit intellectualizing and get down to the nitty-gritty, the gut level, the here-and-now, and then go home with pleasant memories to a routine cosmetic existence.

Sidney Jourard[15]

If people can get fun from these sessions, that's fine. Fun is not a commodity readily available in supermarkets. But let them not kid themselves and us that they are on the road to becoming Ideal New Men, for that is a full-time existence incorporating every area of life.

We would maintain that, although these group experiences can be a powerful generator of intent to develop one's potential, to "get in touch" with oneself and others, they are not essential. The means lie readily to hand for any two people with an ongoing relationship.

We can orbit the earth, touch the moon . . . And yet this society has not devised a way (though love propels our very existence) for man and woman to live together for seven straight days with any assurance of harmony.

George B. Leonard[16]

At a time when most areas of the earth have been fully explored, all mountains climbed and the vastness of space is

15. Jourard, "A Way to Encounter," in *ibid.*
16. "The Man and Woman Thing," *Look,* December 24, 1968.

being reduced, the last frontier to man and woman still remains themselves. They will always be pioneers. And pioneers have a vision, and visions transcend feelings of anonymity, alienation and despair.

Only—but this is rare—
When a beloved hand is laid in ours,
When, jaded with the rush and glare
Of the interminable hours,
Our eyes can in another's eyes read clear,
When our world-deafened ear
Is by the tones of a loved voice caressed—
A bolt is shot back somewhere in our breast,
And a lost pulse of feeling stirs again.
The eye sinks inward, and the heart lies plain,
And what we mean, we say, and what we would, we know.
A man becomes aware of his life's flow . . .

Matthew Arnold

2·Getting in Touch with Each Other

A MARITAL CHECKUP

Prevention has become an increasingly quoted concept in discussions on crime, physical ill health and environmental pollution. We do not wait for things to go wrong; we attempt to anticipate misfortunes and, by appropriate remedial action, prevent catastrophe. Marriage can be looked at in a similar way.

Geologists have recently discovered that this planet consists of a number of "plates" on which the continents and oceans are situated. These plates are in perpetual movement. At the points where plates meet, areas of high tension are created—a situation which provides the potential for earthquakes. Some of these meetings produce a series of minor earthquakes as the plates adjust to each other's physical presence. Where there are no minor disturbances there is a gradual buildup of pressure until an enormous earthquake readjusts their alignment. The intention behind these exercises is to ensure that a series of minor earthquakes is substituted for the major cataclysms, which admittedly do the job of creating change but destroy homes and people as a consequence.

A good marriage can profit from a "checkup." An average marriage has potential for considerable development. A poor marriage has nothing to lose from attempting these exercises.

A WORD OF WARNING

The breakup of a poor marriage could be exacerbated by these exercises. This is a danger and couples should be aware of this before beginning. We do not happen to believe that marital breakdown is always a bad thing. Because of the human misery generated the breakup should always be a step taken as a last resort. Unfortunately, mistakes are made in choosing a partner, or in learning to live together, and in particular in learning to change together. In some of these cases there is no alternative to dissolution other than a lifetime of dissatisfaction. Of course, it is easy for us to talk in the abstract, unaware of the realities and complexities of your relationship. We would personally choose to live a fully charged emotional life and could not tolerate an existence on a permanent voltage reduction. You may feel otherwise—that an inadequate marriage is better for you than no marriage at all. That is your choice.

BEING SERIOUS CAN BE VERY FUNNY

Marriage is a serious business. The consequences of one's actions in marriage are considerable. As with all human situations of potential tension, our culture is rich in jokes and stories about marriage. Although we would hope that anyone doing these exercises would gain something of permanent value for themselves and their marriage, many people have dissolved into laughter when attempting certain exercises. Many of the games are designed as entertainments, and we hope that all of them will provide enjoyment. If this book does no more than cause two people to laugh together then we will feel that our efforts have been justified.

DO WE HAVE TO FOLLOW THESE EXERCISES TO THE LETTER?

No. These are guides only. We have suggested techniques that we think will be of most help, but the more inventive you can be the better.

We have suggested that you write down your answers. This is deliberate as it often allows people to view issues more dispassionately. This is essential if a climate amenable to learning is to be nurtured. Another reason for writing is that it often helps to clarify one's thoughts and feelings.

There are people who don't know what they think about something until they've heard what they had to say.

Peter de Vries

We have insisted on a procedure whereby one person never interrupts another. This we do think is essential. Interrupting is one of the most common causes of irritation, not to mention misunderstanding, in marriages. And, as Kipling noted, "when grown-ups agree they interrupt each other almost as much as if they were quarrelling."

CHANGE AS A STYLE OF LIFE

Since 'tis Nature's law to change,
Constancy alone is strange.

John Wilmot

The opening chapter of this book argued that whether we approve of it or not we live in a highly transient society where change is the order of things. The pressures of society must have their effects on individual relationships, and this, combined with natural maturation, means that adults do change. No marriage can survive unless both partners develop the skills to manage these changes, for they cannot be prevented.

It is hoped that these exercises may furnish some marriages with a blueprint for harmonious change where previously none existed.

The first step is to be clear about what the resistances are to personal growth and change. To help us we can make use of a technique used by social scientists, with the rather off-putting title of "force-field analysis." In simple terms this means looking at all the forces that come to bear on any situation in life when someone wishes to make changes.

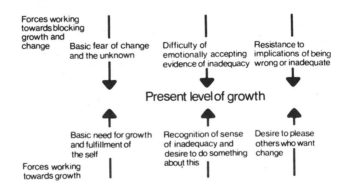

The primary focus of the exercises must be on the concept of the self that every individual possesses. This "self-concept," as it is often referred to, signifies the person that we think we are. Some people like to think of the self as a kind of onion; one peels back layer after layer until one reaches the point where one's eyes begin to water. This is the point at which to

1. Adapted from Edgar H. Schein, "Forces Which Undermine Management Development," *California Management Review*, 5 (Summer 1963), 32.

stop, for this is considered to be the deep underlying self. A concept which we prefer sees the self from a number of different perspectives. A simple model to demonstrate this has been developed by Joseph Luft and Harry Ingram, called, perhaps too cutely, the Jo-Hari Window.[2]

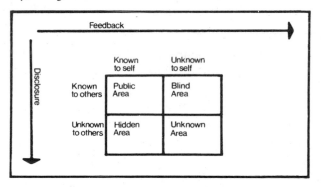

Public area: This refers to those parts of ourselves that we know about and that we are happy for other people to know about.

Blind area: This is the "bad breath" area—those aspects of ourselves that other people see but of which we are blissfully ignorant. Someone may see himself as a gentle, caring man, but those around him know that he is anything but that. Some light needs to be shed through that murky part of the window. Most of us go through life receiving very little feedback from other people about how they see us. Our workmates and friends are usually too polite. One certainly gets feedback of a sort from one's spouse but this is often at the height of a quarrel when its accuracy is perhaps open to question and we are, in any case, unprepared to accept it. These exercises are designed to help spouses give important feedback to one another in a constructive way as part of a wider process of opening up one's public area.

2. Luft discusses their model in greater detail in his book, *Group Processes* (2d ed.), National Press Books, Palo Alto, Calif., 1970.

I have two principal ways of discovering the areas where I fail to see myself. The first is acknowledging the qualities in others which irritate me. The second is recognizing the comments that make me defensive.

Hugh Prather[3]

Hidden area: Most people have parts of themselves that they prefer to keep hidden. They may be ashamed at certain thoughts. "Perhaps," they think, "people will not accept me or love me if they know this about me." We probably keep less hidden from our marriage partner than from anyone else, but most people retain something. Often this hidden part is a burden to us and to disclose it is an important prerequisite to personal growth.

Unknown area: This is sometimes called the "area of potential growth." This is an apt phrase. It refers to the potential we all possess that has not yet come to light. Many of the exercises are designed to unearth and cultivate that potential, in particular the ones concerned with encouraging awareness of one's strengths and of the environment in which one lives.

Caution

Self-disclosure, although a determinant of personal growth, is a process to be undertaken carefully. Self-disclosure must be appropriate to the situation. Clearly, some kinds of disclosure could terminate or severely complicate a marital relationship rather than deepen it.

> Ann had a brief affair with someone while Alan was away. It only lasted a week. She enjoyed it but felt slightly guilty. Her relationship with Alan was very good, although the dailiness of life had rubbed off some of the sparkle. This she

3. *Notes to Myself,* Real People Press, Lafayette, Calif., 1970.

knew was inevitable. She certainly did not want to end her marriage, and neither did she wish to continue having affairs. To her this was simply one spontaneous event that she had no desire to repeat. She hated keeping anything from Alan and felt that the affair should not have any effect on their relationship. She had not changed as a result of it. However, she knew enough about Alan to realize that he could never understand or forgive this.

Was it worth taking the risk of destroying her relationship so that she could feel cleansed by her confession? It is not for us to advise on such a personal decision. We can point out that without a trained counselor in attendance, a confession of this nature can trigger off consequences which partners neither can control nor want.

PROVIDING FEEDBACK

If you are to help your partner understand himself, and vice versa, there are certain things to bear in mind.

What Makes It Difficult for Us to Receive Help?[4]

1. It is difficult enough to admit our faults and problems to ourselves, let alone to someone else. We have to decide if we trust our partner sufficiently. If we are not convinced of this, the lack of trust itself needs to be explored.[5] We are often afraid of what our partner will think about us if he or she knows this terrible thing.

2. We may have worked hard at establishing our independence. Talking in this intimate way might seem like surrendering it. This usually indicates feelings of insecurity in the relationship and the individual's lack of confidence in *being* himself.

4. This list is adapted freely from "Feedback and the Helping Relationship," *NTL Institute: Reading Book*, 1967.
5. The exercises in Chapter 6 provide a framework for this exploration.

3. We may have spent all our lives looking for someone to be dependent on. The danger of this is that such a person does not really want to help himself; he wants the other person to solve all his problems for him.

4. We may be looking for sympathy and support rather than for help to really enable us to tackle a problem.

Confession is often an avoidance of change. If I confess it, I don't have to accept the responsibility of changing it: "I confess. It is beyond my control." And it shifts the burden: "You have heard it, now what are you going to do about it?"

Hugh Prather

---

5. We may feel that our problem is so unique that no one else could really understand it. We will never know, of course, until we try.

6. On the other hand, we may feel that our problem is so commonplace that it would make us look silly to talk about it.

What Makes It Difficult to Give Help to Others?

1. Most of us like to give advice. It makes us feel important. In the eighteenth century, the Earl of Chesterfield commented that "advice is seldom welcome; and those who want it the most always want it the least." Two hundred years later it is our experience that the last thing people seek from others is advice. They may ask for it, but you will not be well regarded if you are tempted to provide it. If you are really pushed hard by someone for your opinion on a problem, then this can be given, so long as it is prefaced with words to the effect that "Telling you what I would do will not really help you. We are different people, and the world looks different to both of us. Because of that I could never have *your problem*.

It would automatically be different for me—it would be *my problem*. I can say what I would do in similar circumstances. But I am not you."

When one person is trying to help another person solve a problem, he will be most effective if he acts as a *facilitator*, not as a provider of solutions. He should facilitate the individual's own thinking around his problems, rather than try to solve them for him. People can solve only their own problems and never those of anyone else. When someone attempts to solve a problem of yours, you will often feel slightly irritated. This is because in doing this he has "taken over" your problem. We are jealous of our problems and guard against "takeovers," while being more open to "mergers," where two minds jointly consider the problem. However, unlike a business merger, one of the partners is firmly in control of any possible action, and that is the problem owner.

2. If someone suddenly says something with which we disagree violently, we are often tempted to *argue*. As soon as this happens we are not helping that person. We are now attempting to satisfy our own needs instead of theirs. If someone becomes aggressive or obstructive, find out why he is acting in that way instead of simply reacting to it.

3. In trying to create a climate in which problems can be explored, the temptation is sometimes to agree vigorously with everything that is said. This, along with excessive praise, can be somewhat disconcerting if the person is doubtful of some of his views or behavior. The climate that is likely to be of most help to a person seeking help is one in which you are saying in effect, "No matter what you do I will *love* you and *help* you, but I will not necessarily *like* everything that you do." Accepting a person is not the same as agreeing with everything he does or says. The renowned psychotherapist Carl Rogers expresses this very well. "What I am describing is a feeling which is not paternalistic, nor sentimental, nor superficially social and agreeable. It respects the other person

as a separate individual, and does not possess him. It is a kind of liking which has strength, and which is not demanding." He calls it *positive regard*.

4. It is easy to deny the feelings of the person we are trying to help. This is done in all sorts of subtle ways—"You can't possibly believe that!" or "Everybody has problems like that" —in other words, his problem is nothing special. To make people feel happier we say, "But you have no reason to feel that way," when, as far as he is concerned, he has every reason for feeling that way. Spouses commonly report a lack of understanding which is traced to this tendency. A wife says how unhappy she is. Her husband says, "You can't be unhappy, you've a good home, fine children, and a husband who loves you."

5. Most of us have a system of defenses which prevents us from getting hurt or from experiencing excessive guilt about parts of ourselves that we find unacceptable. Sometimes these defenses are only too obvious to someone we live with. If you know that your partner is hiding behind an elaborate network of defenses then it is sometimes tempting to knock them down, leaving him naked and exposed. These shock tactics do sometimes work, but they are risky. It is safer to build up a climate of trust and understanding so that your partner feels able to emerge from behind those defenses of his own free will.

6. Do not psychoanalyze. You may be able to dazzle your partner with brilliant insights into the causes of his problems. You might stagger him with a virtuoso performance gleaned from your paperback Freud, but it is unlikely that you will help him. To be told that his present problem of relating to women is due to an unsuccessful resolution of his Oedipus complex and from living with an aggressive sister who could not come to terms with her penis envy is likely to confound him and leave him more confused than before you started. If he came up with that explanation himself, then it would

mean something. The fact that it comes from you tends to negate its usefulness.

Our partner can best cast light on our window into the self by appropriate feedback of his impression and reactions. However, there are more or less useful ways of providing this feedback:

Ensure that any feedback is descriptive rather than evaluative. Say, "You seem very anxious when you talk about your boss," rather than, "I don't know why you don't confront your boss about your pay."

Make any feedback specific. Telling your wife that she is "domineering" is likely to antagonize her because she will not understand to which aspects of her behavior you are referring. Instead, your response should be specific: "When you talk to me in the way that you just did, I feel that you are trying to order me around and this makes me angry." This is instant feedback on a piece of her behavior and she knows just what you are referring to.

Feedback can be destructive if the person is not in any position to do anything about the problem. If you think your wife is ugly, telling her this will not be very constructive! Frustration is only increased when a person is reminded of some shortcoming over which he has no control.

Feedback is rarely welcomed unless it is asked for.

It is essential to check that your partner has really heard the feedback you have been giving. Distortion is very common, especially on emotionally loaded topics like our own behavior. In brief, any helping relationship between two people demands:

- Mutual trust.
- Recognition that the helping situation is a *joint exploration* of a problem.
- Concentration and effective listening, with the helper doing more listening than his partner.

- Following up what his partner says, rather than one's own insights into the problem.
- The helper should constantly check out his perceptions of what his partner has been saying and is feeling.

PREPARING FOR THE EXERCISES

Intending to complete these exercises is all very well but, in a busy life, especially a family life with children's needs to be met, the intention is often difficult to accomplish. One way is to set aside a special evening, similar to an outing to a club, theater or restaurant. If either partner feels harassed because of other demands, it is best to postpone the evening. Make sure the children are in bed or in some other way well removed from their parents' strange antics!

INTRODUCTION TO THE EXERCISES

Some of the main problems in marriage are lack of trust, poor communication and inadequate knowledge about oneself and one's partner. The following chapters, it is hoped, will be beneficial to a developing relationship but are also geared toward personal growth and an increased sensitivity toward oneself, one's partner, and the world about one.

We have used slogans liberally to emphasize points. The aim is either to elicit shock which will lead to further thought or to crystallize an argument that has been developed. Readers may like to create their own slogans as they work their way through the games and exercises.

In Iris Murdoch's novel *Under the Net,* one of the leading characters says, "I have solitude, but I'm afraid of intimacy. The substance of my life is a private conversation with myself which to turn into a dialogue would be equivalent to self-destruction." It is our hope that through the following exercises, you will discover or confirm for yourselves that

intimacy need not be likened to a praying mantis but is a
condition which can facilitate maximum individual growth
in a climate which has as its basis acceptance, affection and
security.

3·Discovering One Another

Self-knowledge is best learned, not by contemplation, but action.
Goethe

Before becoming a fully qualified electrician, the apprentice has to know all there is to know about the tools he will use in his work. The salesman must be fully conversant with the products he is selling. The politician needs to be well versed in party dogma and policies. The only resource that someone can bring to his marriage is himself. If the electrician did not understand his tools we would not ask him into our house. Yet many of us enter marriage without knowledge of the basic equipment—namely, ourselves.

To thine own self be true
And it must follow, as the night the day,
Thou canst not then be false to any man.

The advice of Polonius to Laertes cited above can only be followed if the self is an open book to the reader, who can quote from it chapter and verse. Unlike a book, however, which remains static while its owner peruses its contents, the self changes before the reader's eyes. Indeed, the very act of reading often results in a new edition.

This chapter is aimed at opening the shutters to reveal all four panes of the Jo-Hari Window. By following the exercises systematically you will be able to define your public self, obtain information on the area of the self to which you are blind, and by sharing aspects of your hidden self, will discover new data about who you are and what you want to be. The exercises are based on the assumption that two people can get to know themselves best through sharing their perceptions of themselves and of one another.

IT TAKES TWO TO SEE ONE
Samuel Culpert[1]

These exercises will help to answer three questions:

Who am *I*?
Who do *you* see when you look at me?
How can *we* help each other to develop as people?

WHO AM I?

This is a question which has always been central to man's awareness of his own existence. Socrates taught "Know thyself" as a prerequisite to any solution of a human dilemma. In advanced societies where man's basic needs for food, water, warmth and safety are diverting less and less of his daily energy, he increasingly confronts himself with questions about his own identity. Yet one of the sad facts of our age, as witnessed by countless novels, films and plays, is that when a man is free to confront himself he discovers all too often that

1. "The Interpersonal Process of Self-disclosure: It Takes Two to See One," in *Sensitivity Training and the Laboratory Approach,* ed. Robert T. Golembiewski and Arthur Blumberg, Peacock, Franklin Park, Ill., 1970.

he is looking at a stranger. What is more, he needs an introduction to that stranger. Contemporary man has to rediscover
the ability to communicate with himself. The Eastern philosophers have always felt more comfortable with this process
than Western man, who is not merely afraid of his own reflection but is often terrified by his own substance.

The exercises in this section are aimed at helping you to
get in touch with yourself: your feelings, beliefs, values and
body. There may be some surprise at seeing the word "body"
included. But we believe that knowledge of ourselves includes all perimeters of the self, and that includes the body,
which in modern Western society is often misunderstood or
completely ignored. We talk of "body odor" instead of "body
perfumes." The smells of our armpits, skin, breath and pubic
area have been banished to the dollar-lined waste baskets in
the ad agency's basement. Instead of coming to terms with
what Nature has provided us with, we aim to suppress it. We
want to introduce you to your body. That is the first step
toward accepting that it belongs to you, that it is something
you can trust in and learn from, and over which you can
exercise a large measure of control.

EXERCISE 1: *Allow Me to Introduce Myself to Me*
Approximate time = one hour

Both partners should carry out the following activities independently. After completion you can share your observations.

1. Imagine that you are to be programed into a computer for
   eternity. This means that at any time, by tapping out the
   appropriate code, you will receive a printout which will describe exactly the sort of person you are. Because of limitations
   on computer time and storage space you are only allowed to
   place ten statements about yourself into the computer.
   You are to write down the ten statements that will convey

to anyone who does not know you the picture that best sums you up. These ten statements should enable anyone to say, "Yes, well now that I know these things, I think that I can understand what it feels like to be John Smith." These statements could range from simple statements of fact such as "I am six feet and two inches tall," to more complex ones such as "On finding myself in a new situation with people I don't know I have a tendency to . . ."

You must use your allotted computer storage space, that is, make ten statements, but you can make no more than ten statements.

2. Imagine that you wear your statements like clothes which are exhibited to a watching world, with the least revealing on the outside. You are now to participate in a striptease. *You are to number your ten statements from one to ten in terms of which is to be stripped off first.* You should be left with the statement which reveals most about yourself.

3. Share your statements and their ranking with your partner, who shares his with you. Just listen, do not make any comment.

EXERCISE 2: *Your Obituary*
Approximate time = one hour

The (London) *Times* has an obituary column in which the deaths of Very Important People are reported with a descriptive account of their lives and an evaluation from the obituarist.

You are to imagine that you have just died, and your life is to be written about in exactly the same manner as *The Times* obituary. This does not mean, of course, that you must have been a VIP in society's eyes.

1. Describe your life up until your death. You do not have to die now. You should describe your entire life, even if it ends many years from now.

2. Describe your death and state your age at death.
3. Ask yourself the question: "Does this description sum up what I want from my life?"
4. If the last answer was "yes," then no further comment is necessary. If the answer is "no," then describe how *ideally* you would like the obituary to read.
5. Make up an epitaph which you feel would succinctly sum up: (a) the life you have led and expect to lead, and (b) the life you would like to lead.
6. Share your obituary and epitaph with your partner. Do not comment on your partner's contributions.

EXERCISE 3: *Peak and Trough Experiences*
Approximate time = forty-five minutes

Ionesco made the point that many people have delusions of grandeur but some are deluded by triviality. This is an exercise which aims at an escape from life's trivia.

1. Write down any event or series of events which you have experienced which you would call *peak experiences*. These refer to the high spots of your life. Those times which in themselves seem to justify living. (a) Say what it was, (b) describe what happened, and (c) discuss your feelings about it.
2. Write down any event or series of events which you have experienced which you would call *trough experiences*. These refer to the low spots of your life—those times when life hardly seemed worth living.
3. Share your experiences without comment.

EXERCISE 4: *Commentary Time*
Approximate time = could be anything

The previous three exercises should have resulted in a large amount of data being shared. You have been encouraged to re-

strain yourselves from comment. Married couples so often interrupt or do not really listen to each other, so that these exercises
have been designed to allow one-way communication only. Now
is the time to see the value of permitting your partner to be
himself.

1. John summarizes what he has heard Jill say about herself in
   the previous three exercises. He asks Jill if his summary is
   accurate. If it is not, then she should point out any inaccu-
   racies.
2. John comments on anything that he has heard (a) which was
   new information to him, (b) which surprised him, and (c)
   which has affected his attitudes or feelings toward Jill.
3. Jill repeats this procedure in relation to John.

EXERCISE 5: *My Hero and Heroine*
Approximate time = thirty minutes

A person's heroes often reflect his ambitions if not his actual
self. Consequently, this exercise, while providing considerable
enjoyment, can be very enlightening. The first five parts are to be
done independently.

1. Choose four people, past or present, male or female, who come
   closest to your idea of "heroes."
2. Why do you choose these people to be heroes? In our experience, while women often choose men as their heroes, men
   seldom choose women. If this happens, when you complete this
   exercise it might be useful to discuss why you think that this
   has happened.
3. Which person, living or dead, would you most like to be, and
   why?
4. Which four people do you think your partner might have
   chosen, and why?

5. Which person do you think your partner would most like to be, and why?
6. One of you should share your heroes with the other partner along with the reasons for your choice.
7. Your partner is to comment on how predictable these are, and whether he is surprised at any of your choices.
8. Your partner then reads out to you the heroes he had picked "for you," with the reasons for his choices. You can comment on these.
9. The procedure is now repeated as your partner reads out his selection to you and listens to your reactions and predictions.

EXERCISE 6: *What Do the Newspapers Say about You?*
Approximate time = however long it takes you to read a newspaper

We sometimes like to convince ourselves that we are someone we are not. This represents the public image that we present to the world. We maintain something which may be false in order not only to impress others, but often to impress ourselves too.

1. Each partner takes two or three daily newspapers (from different days) and reads them as he would normally read them. *Note:* If you really want to get the most out of this you should read through a newspaper now before reading any more about the exercise. This exercise is designed to find out where your interests really lie rather than where you would like to think they lie.
2. After reading the same newspapers, sit down with your partner and go through them page by page asking him what he has read. This must be done honestly if you really want to discover what it is you actually read. In our experience, couples are sometimes very surprised by what their partners do, and perhaps more to the point, do not, read.

Allow Me to Introduce My Body . . .
Approximate time = probably a minimum of one hour

When people are asked to locate themselves, their feeling of "me" or self within their bodies, they invariably point to a spot roughly two inches behind their eyeballs. For many people this seems to sum up their feelings about their bodies, which are seen merely as appendages which begin where their necks end.

This exercise is designed to help you discover just how well you know your own body. The requirements are a long mirror, a hand mirror, a very warm room and uninterrupted privacy. (You may not relish explaining to children or friends just why you are lying stark naked on the living-room carpet!)

Man has no Body distinct from his Soul; for that called Body is a portion of Soul discerned by the five senses, the chief inlets of Soul in this age.

William Blake

---

1. It is best if both partners are naked. If one person is naked and his partner is fully clothed, the feeling is something akin to that arising from arriving in jeans and a sweater to what turns out to be a formal dinner party.
2. Whoever is to describe himself first lies down on the floor or bed. You are to close your eyes. Imagine that your body is a geographical area and that you are a surveyor, mapping out this new territory for the first time. Begin at your feet and work your way up to the top of your head, describing in as much detail as possible everything that is to be seen. If you have a tape recorder this should ideally be recorded. The description should be carried out with your eyes still closed. As you describe the "terrain," your partner follows the journey

53

with his eyes, noting any part of the territory that is missed or described inaccurately. *Note:* Remember that you have two sides, a front and a back. This will necessitate some turning around to enable your partner to see everything which you describe.

3. After the description is complete, you should now stand before a full-length mirror, while the tape is played back. Look for the things you have missed or misrepresented. There may be parts of your rear view that you have never seen. This is where the combination of your partner and the hand mirror will reflect light on these unexplored regions. Many women have never really been able to examine their genital region closely, nor men to see the area between their testicles and backside. Here is the opportunity to do so. If no tape recording has been made, your partner should consult his notes as together you describe your body from toe to top.

We should point out that when doing this exercise, many people crack up with laughter, while others find it so erotic that they never complete it. Although the exercise does not set out specifically to produce ribaldry, if it does nothing else we feel that it will have brought something to your relationship.

4. The exercise is repeated with the surveyor now becoming the observer of his partner's "territory."
5. Discuss what, if anything, surprised you about either your own body or your partner's body. We have found that some people find that they have looked, not just at their own, but also at their partner's body for the first time.

EXERCISE 8: *The Body Swap Shop*
Approximate time = thirty minutes

This should follow directly from Exercise 7. It is designed to elicit your feelings about your body.

1. You are to imagine that you can exchange any part of your body for something different. (Remember that your body includes your head.) What parts would you exchange? Why? What would you want the replacements to look like?

   Each partner is to write down the answers to these independently. Before writing about any part, examine it carefully, using the mirrors.
2. Try to guess what parts of the body your partner might wish to change, and say what you think his reasons might be.
3. Exchange information with one another.
4. Tell your partner which parts of his body you like best and why.

EXERCISE 9: *Controlling Your Body*
Approximate time = thirty minutes to one hour

Not only are many people uncertain about what their bodies look like but they have also forgotten what their bodies feel like. We are aware of the extreme feelings that no one can miss like headaches, orgasms, indigestion and itches, but we miss the more subtle happenings which characterize our body's being.

This exercise is intended to alert you to the way different muscle systems feel. It is also designed as a method for reducing anxiety through relaxation. As such, we feel this is valuable in itself. This also demonstrates that you can control your body so that it can help you psychologically. Sufficient medical evidence exists to show how bodily states influence one's emotions and thinking and vice versa. The message is that if you can achieve bodily relaxation then you will also have a relaxed mind. But to control your body you need to know it.

The rationale behind this exercise is that when muscles are tensed, and then relaxed, they enter into a deeper state of relaxation than if you try only to relax them.

If a tape recorder is available, the following instructions can be recorded and both partners can relax simultaneously. If not, one partner should help the other to relax by reading out the instructions. The timing of these instructions is vital. They should be read out slowly, in a soft voice, allowing a number of seconds to pass before moving from one instruction to another. Watch your partner closely to gauge when you think he is ready for you to move on.

BODY RELAXATION INSTRUCTIONS

"I want you to lie down on the floor. Let yourself be loose. Let your limbs choose for themselves where they want to lie. Let your head roll into a position that feels right. You are now going to rid your body of tensions, starting at your feet. Enter into them. See if you can discover any tenseness. If you can, let it escape from your feet. That tension would really rather be out than imprisoned in there. If your feet are now relaxed, move up to your ankles. Search out any tenseness that you can find lurking in those bones. You are traveling up your legs now. You can feel the muscles at the back of your legs. But you don't want to be able to feel them. Forget that you have muscles there. From your waist down you have no legs, only lumps of jelly with no feeling. Search out any feeling in your legs and let it escape from the jelly. Your legs are now relaxed. . . .

"Take a few deep breaths and begin to feel tension sliding out of the rest of your body. Your arms and hands might feel twitchy. Let them twitch. They are just getting rid of tension. Listen to your own breathing. Go with it. You can trust it. It's never let you down in the past. Ease the tension out of your back. It wants to escape—let it. Your chest and back are now relaxed. Your arms and hands are loose. Your head feels comfortable. Let your jaw do what it wants to do. Let your cheek muscles slacken. If your eyelids want to close, let them close. If they want to remain open, let them stay open. Your scalp is comfortable. It is just flowing gently over the top of your head—like cream poured onto a baked apple. Your body is now relaxed. Feel the relaxation and wallow in it. Let it flow over you like the silent joy of anticipated sleep. Stay with the feeling. . . ."

(Let your partner stay relaxed for half a minute or more before continuing.)

"I want you to concentrate on your hands now. I want you to clench your fists tightly. Feel the power of your fists. The power is beginning to move up your arms. Your arms are feeling the tension rising up. Raise your arms above your head. You are still clenching your fists tightly. Hold your arms there. . . ."

(Let your partner stay like this for about ten seconds.)

"Now let your arms drop to the floor. Relax your fists. Let your fingers do what they want to do. Note the difference between the feelings of tension which you felt a few seconds ago, and the feelings of relaxation you feel now in your hands and arms.

"We are now going to concentrate on the muscles in your forearms. Push your hands up in the air again, only this time pushing your hands forward so that you are looking at the backs of your hands. Push hard. Feel the tension in your forearms. Hold it like that. . . .

"Now let them drop back to the floor. Notice the feelings of relaxation in your forearms.

"That's good. We are now going to concentrate on the muscles in your upper arms. Bend your arms at the elbow so that your hands are up in the air. Now flex your biceps until I tell you to stop. . . ."

(Allow about ten seconds.)

"Right, let them relax, notice how the feeling of relaxation spreads through your fingertips.

"We are going to concentrate on your head now. Let's concentrate on the muscles in your forehead. Wrinkle your forehead by raising your eyebrows. Hold them like that. . . ."

(Allow ten seconds.)

"Relax. Notice how smooth your forehead feels as all these muscles smooth out.

"It is now time for the area surrounding your eyes and nose. Close your eyes more and more tightly while I count up to ten. . . . Relax, keeping your eyes closed. Enjoy the soothing feeling, just like it sometimes feels when you close your eyes after you have been feeling tired for some time.

"Next we are going to work on the area surrounding your lips, cheeks and jaw. You are going to give the widest grin that you have ever managed. It will stretch from ear to ear. Hold that for a while. . . ."

(Allow ten seconds.)

"Relax. See how loose your cheeks and lips feel. Let your jaw hang. Appreciate the feeling.

"Now swallow hard and hold that swallow. Feel the tenseness in your throat muscles. . . . Relax. Let your neck hang loose.

"As you continue to relax further and further, notice how your breathing has become more and more regular.

"We will now concentrate on the shoulder muscles. Raise your shoulders to try to touch your ears. Keep them tense. Feel the tension rippling through the muscles."

(Allow ten seconds.)

"Now relax. Let your shoulders slump, and notice the warm, tingling ripples that are now in your muscles. Let the tingling spread through your arms and reach your fingertips.

"We move next to your stomach muscles. Pull your stomach muscles in as far as they will go."

(Allow ten seconds.)

"Relax. Visualize your muscles falling back into place around one another. Notice how they move in time to your breathing, which is regular and relaxed.

"We will next go to the muscles in your thighs. Bend your legs and simultaneously bend your toes backward as you draw your knees toward your chin. Feel the tension in your thighs."

(Allow five seconds.)

"Relax. There is a warm, tingling feeling moving down toward your toes. Let it reach them.

"Once again, bend your legs but this time bend your toes

away from your head, tensing your calf muscles. Visualize the muscles fibers taut and stretched. . . ."

(Allow five seconds.)

"Relax. Your legs and feet feel no tension now. There is no tension throughout your body. You are now even more relaxed than when we started. Concentrate on all the muscle areas as I mention them and feel how relaxed they are . . . see if you can relax them even more.

"Your forehead . . . eyes and nose . . . chin and mouth . . . throat . . . shoulders . . . upper arms . . . forearms . . . hands . . . stomach . . . feel the wave of relaxation spreading down to your thighs . . . calf muscles . . . feet . . . to the tips of your toes.

"You have been relaxing very well. That beautiful, relaxed tone to your body is now to be replaced by new energy which will activate your total system. I am going to count backward from five to one and when I reach the count of one you will have your eyes open and feel quite refreshed and calm. It is important to stretch out all your limbs to see if you can get them to fall apart like a cat does after sleep. Then you will *slowly* get up. Are you ready . . . 5—4—3—2—1. Now stretch and rise up very slowly."

Many people find this exercise both relaxing and invigorating. It moves from relaxing the person with no tension to a deliberate buildup of tension in selected muscle areas to gradual relaxation. The final relaxation following the tension-producing actions is usually much deeper than the initial relaxation achieved. This serves to emphasize the point that tension followed by relaxation is for most people the more effective method. It is hoped that the exercise gives people the confidence to use their body to gain mental relaxation and the ability to be able to control their muscles to achieve this.[2]

2. For those interested in pursuing further techniques of body relaxation and control, consult Bernard Gunther's book *Sense Relaxation*, Macmillan, New York, 1968.

WHO DO YOU SEE WHEN YOU LOOK AT ME?

People spend hours making up their faces, adjusting ties and pocket handkerchiefs, combing hair. We assume that the image that we see in our mirror is also what others see. But we only see half of what they see—the front half. From time to time we wonder whether our hair looks as good at the back as we think it does at the front. We make sure that no slip is showing, and we clean the backs of our shoes (though rarely with the ferocity that ensures a glistening toe end). But generally, we still assume that their visual image of us is equivalent to our own image. The remarks that we make behind other people's backs should suggest that remarks are perhaps made behind *our* backs also. Just as others see behind our physical "front," so they see behind the social "front."

We pass through life rarely acquiring information from others about what they think of the image that we are projecting. From time to time, often in arguments, through friendships more rarely, other people tell us what they think of us. This is not usually very helpful: "You're a damned fool," "How childish you are," "I think you're marvelous." The sum of what these statements tell us about a person's behavior is nil. Yet it is exactly this type of comment that is typical of a close relationship, the very relationship that should be capable of providing some of the most important information on how you look to other people. The exercises in this section are all designed with the intention of maximizing the constructive feedback from your partner on the image you present to him and others.

EXERCISE 1: *What Are My Strengths?*
Approximate time = one hour

We live in a society where, for the most part, if you are performing efficiently no one says a word, but the moment that you do something wrong there is immediate criticism. Much of United States management is run (or misrun) on the simple dictum that too much praise makes Johnny smug and lazy while complaints and criticism keep him on his toes. The psychological evidence on this is quite clear. The majority of people respond positively to praise, especially from significant people in their lives. A few people also respond positively to criticism with an "I'll show him" attitude. But for the most part, people are depressed by criticism rather than invigorated.

This cultural hangup manifests itself in our personal relationships. Many people find it difficult to express their feelings toward someone else, especially if those feelings are positive. This is reciprocated by the person on the receiving end of this praise. If someone verbally attacks us in a vicious and potentially wounding manner, we know how to deal with it: we stand up and give back as good (or as bad) as we have received. But if someone sincerely praises us we collapse into a heap of embarrassed, mumbling, tearful, jelly.

WE CAN COPE WITH VIOLENCE BUT WE ARE STILL LEARNING TO COPE WITH LOVE

Trainers of sensitivity (training) groups commonly report that many people find it difficult to talk about what they are good at, but can participate at length in searching self-criticism and abuse. Many people find that one of life's most difficult tasks is the challenge of being able to love oneself. Unfortunately, too much clinical evidence has accumulated which demonstrates clearly that people who have little self-esteem are likely to be very unhappy, depressed and persistently dissatisfied and to have a low regard for others.

TO BE ABLE TO LOVE OTHERS YOU MUST FIRST LEARN TO LOVE YOURSELF

Although this exercise is concerned with providing you with personal feedback from your partner, it is also designed to force you to think about the strong points about yourself. So many people lack a vocabulary for expressing self-praise that we are going to suggest one for you.

1. Both partners write down the answer to the following questions: "What are my strengths?" "What potential strengths do I have and what is keeping me from using these strengths?"

2. Before proceeding consult the following list of areas where you and your partner may have strengths. We sometimes think of personal strengths in a restricted way. This list is designed as a mental trigger to remind you of the many areas you might consider. It is not an exhaustive list.

AREAS OF PERSONAL STRENGTHS

a. *Intellectual strengths:* Ability to solve problems. Intellectual curiosity. Ability to quickly pick up plots of films, plays and books; to express ideas coherently; to accept new ideas. Ability to think in an original and creative way. Persistence in solving a problem. Ability to make decisions in a rational, balanced manner, by carefully weighing the alternatives.

b. *Special abilities:* Ability to add sums quickly in your head. Ability to write clearly. Mechanical ability. Ability to work well with your hands in constructing or repairing things; to persuade others about the value of a product or idea; to talk easily to a variety of people. Ability to make the best of your appearance, by means of grooming or choice of clothes; to manage finance, to speak in public, to make plants grow, to cook well, to climb mountains. Knowledge of languages.

c. *Educational strengths:* What are your educational achievements at primary school, secondary school, any other full-time or part-time education? Any training received through your employment? Any self-education through courses and reading?

d. *Vocational strengths:* What jobs have you had? Any positions of responsibility? What satisfactions have you achieved from your work—material rewards, security, companionship, prestige, variety, stimulation, enjoyment of exercising a skill or range of skills, sense of doing something important for the society in which you live, promotion? What special abilities have you displayed at work, *e.g.*, ability to organize, ability to make decisions quickly, persistence, conscientiousness? Are you quick at your job, quick at noticing mistakes? Is your time-keeping good? Do you get along well with others? Can you make things, sell things, repair things, write well, speak effectively, handle groups or committees efficiently?

e. *Interests:* If you have interests, these are an important aspect of your personality strengths.

What activities do you enjoy doing—reading, making things, being with other people, solving puzzles and problems, selling objects or ideas, outdoor activities, helping people, listening to or playing music, watching plays, films, television documentaries, writing? Knowledge of languages, etc.

Do you have any particular activity which you would call a hobby—*e.g.*, gardening, pottery, painting, designing things, constructive activities, jewelry making, reading, sports, politics? What interests do you have in which you invest some of your time?

f. *Aesthetic strengths:* Do you enjoy paintings, books, buildings, furniture and textile design, poetry, drama, films, the countryside or cities? What beauty have you discovered in nature and in people? Do you use your aesthetic sense in the home or at

63

your place of employment? Can you dance, sketch, write, sculpt? Do you play or listen to music, sing, make things with an aesthetic appeal? Do you enjoy choosing clothes?

g. *Social strengths:* Do you help other people? Are you engaged in voluntary social work? Do you belong to local community organizations? Are you politically active? Do you belong to a religious organization? Do you hold any positions of responsibility in these organizations? Are you a blood donor? Do you make friends easily?

h. *Sports and outdoor activities:* Are you good at certain sports? Do you enjoy outdoor activities, *e.g.,* camping, walking, visiting places of historical interest or beauty, traveling abroad?

i. *Health:* Good health represents a strength. What do you do to help maintain your health—medical and dental checkups, any exercise, or attention to diet?

j. *Relationship strengths:* Are you able to meet people easily and make them feel comfortable, to talk easily to strangers? Do you have good relationships with your relatives, neighbors and workmates? Do you treat people with consideration and respect? Are you prepared to trust people, able to really listen to what people say? Can you relate to people, regardless of sex, race, religion or social class? Are you able to risk yourself with new people? Do you have a good sense of humor? Can you express yourself physically with people?

k. *Emotional strengths:* Are you able to give love and to receive it, capable of a wide range of emotions and able to express them freely? Are you capable of spontaneity, able to put yourself into someone else's shoes? Are you aware of your own emotions, able to live with yourself instead of in spite of yourself? Are you able to understand other people's emotions and why they have these feelings?

l. *Domestic strengths:* Are you able to communicate with your spouse, your children? Do you choose to spend time with your family? Do you enjoy family outings, outings alone with your spouse? Do you share domestic responsibilities and activities? Do you express physical affection to your spouse and to your children? Do you feel responsibilities to your parents and other relatives, share decision making in the home? Do you buy spontaneous presents or provide surprise "treats" for your spouse/children? Are you honest with your spouse/children?

Remember that this list is not intended to be exhaustive. It should be a stimulus to thinking about yourself and your partner.

You are now to list all the strengths which you feel your partner possesses and demonstrates. You are to list also any potential strengths which you feel your partner has and your ideas on what blocks are preventing those strengths from being used.

3. You now have a list of the strengths and potential strengths of yourself and your partner. You are now to share your strengths and potential strengths with your partner. Ask for his comments.

   Now ask him what strengths and potential strengths *he* thinks you have.

   Discuss the blockages that either of you mention which are felt to inhibit a potential strength.

4. Repeat this last procedure, but this time your partner is to read out his list of his own strengths and potential strengths and you are to share with him your conclusions about these.

It is now hoped that both of you will have a considerably larger list of strengths than you created for yourself in the first stage of this exercise. You should also have some indication of strengths which either you or your partner feel you possess, but which are blocked.

We now wish to concentrate on these blockages and see how they might be removed. The problem must be tackled by both partners working together to see what actions can be prescribed which the partner in question must carry out. Some examples will best describe what can be achieved.

Bill felt that he had few friends. His wife, Joan, agreed with him, yet could not understand why. Bill was outwardly very friendly, sociable, a marvelous father, and an excellent companion to Joan. Bill was not satisfied with his situation. During their discussion Bill came to realize that he had no real friend apart from Joan. The reason was that he found so much fulfillment at home with Joan and their three children that he made no effort to spend any time with colleagues at work, or anyone else. They both agreed that this was somewhat undesirable.[3] Bill thought of the men that he knew; without exception, they were his work colleagues. He could name at least two with whom he felt that he could become very friendly. Each of them had occasionally suggested that Bill should have a drink with them on the way home after work. Bill resolved to invite them both to have a drink the following week. One of them belonged to a tennis club that he had invited Bill to join. Bill decided to take up the offer, especially as this coincided with another of his "blockages"—relating to his health. Joan had commented that Bill was not as physically fit as he could be and that some regular exercise would help him.

Anne felt that she was not as attractive as she could be. After much hesitation, Alan, her husband, agreed with her. The blockage appeared to have been brought about after their first child was born. Anne had been depressed for some time after the birth and had lost all interest in her appearance. After her depression had lifted there still seemed to be no good reason for wearing attractive clothes. The baby was often sick after feeding or when Anne was playing with the child on the floor. Anne's uniform became shapeless sweaters

3. Whether it is or not is not for us to discuss. The only thing that matters is that Bill and Joan thought this situation to be an unhealthy one.

and practical washable slacks. She resolved to wear make-up again on most days, and at least for two days a week to wear a dress instead of slacks. This was designed to coincide with days when she visited friends with her child. The inevitable happened. Anne began to feel more attractive, always the vital factor, and Alan began to see her as being more attractive. What had begun as the chore of making up and having extra clothes to clean became a habit which did not add much time to her week's work.

EXERCISE 2: *Images*
Approximate time = fifteen minutes

This is usually found to be one of the most enjoyable of these exercises. It can cause so much hilarity that it is easy to miss important information generated by the game. The objective is to shed more light on the public image we present—but that part about which we are rather hazy. The blind area of the self can be explored by this seemingly simple party game.

The exercise consists of each person in turn answering the following questions about his partner: If your partner was to be a motor car what make or model would he be? and why . . .?

This can be played using any image that comes to mind. We have used a variety of images including items of food, drinks, types of buildings, animals and articles of clothing.

EXERCISE 3: *Spirals*
Approximate time = one hour

R. D. Laing, in his book on interpersonal perception,[4] points out that human beings are constantly thinking about others, and about what others are thinking about them, and what others think they are thinking about the others, and so on *ad infinitum*.

4. R. D. Laing, H. Phillipson and A. R. Lee, *Interpersonal Perception*, Springer, New York, 1966.

People do not just act in the ways they want to act. They are often governed by how they think others will see their actions. This problem can lead to a couple developing a "spiral" in their relationship.

Andrew loves Pauline.

Pauline loves Andrew.

Andrew is not sure if Pauline loves him because Pauline tries to boss him.

Pauline is not sure if Andrew loves her because he seems sullen so much of the time at home.

Andrew is sullen because he feels Pauline wants to boss him around.

Pauline feels that Andrew does not want to help her make household decisions—when she asks him he gets sullen.

When Pauline asks Andrew to make up his mind about what school their child should attend, Andrew feels that Pauline has made up her mind already and just wants to force her decision on him. Anyway, he does not see that it has much to do with him. So he is sullen.

When Andrew is sullen it reminds Pauline of her father, who never helped her mother physically in the house or with making any family decisions. Pauline is determined that she does not want a husband like that, so she makes Andrew participate.

Andrew sees Pauline trying to boss him.

Pauline sees Andrew as sullen, like her father.

Andrew is afraid that Pauline does not love him and so gets more sullen.

Pauline is afraid that Andrew does not love her because he is becoming more sullen, and she makes more of an effort to involve him in her life.

And Andrew gets more frightened.

And Pauline gets more frightened.

Yet they really do love one another.

"Stop the spiral we want to get off."

From this example it is possible to see what a spiral is and how it develops.

The only way to stop it is to unwind the spiraling coils. Someone has to take the risk that the survival of the relationship does not depend on this spiral form. Pauline might discover that Andrew really does *not* love her. It is this fear which sparks off the spiraling nature of the relationship. But unless someone takes this risk, the spiral will only tighten and take the couple further and further from the original problem, which in our example is the difference between the couple's expectations of the role of the husband in family decision making. This is a difficult enough problem in itself. A couple have a better chance of finding a solution if they can work from a basis of mutual love, as they could have done in our case study.

This exercise is dedicated to Laing, who has done so much in the past few years to force people to reexamine their own bases of perception.

Each partner answers the following questions independently and writes down the answers.

1. What sort of person am I?[5]
2. What sort of person is my partner?
3. What sort of person does my partner think I am? This will enable you to see whether your image of yourself is the same as your partner's image of you.
4. What sort of image does my partner think I have of myself? This provides a check as to whether your partner really does understand you. For example, you may think he thinks you feel inferior and you may not feel this at all. Result—a misunderstanding of some of your motives.
5. Examine your perceptions of each other. This is best done by

5. This will be a familiar task to those who have already completed Exercise 1 of the "Who Am I?" section of this chapter.

one person at a time. You first read out your self-description (1) without comment or interruption. Your partner then reads out his description of you (2). Discuss the differences and similarities. Then repeat for your partner. Then you read out (3) and compare it with your partner's (2) to see how accurate is your perception of your partner's understanding of you. This is also discussed and repeated for your partner. You read out (4), which will elicit how accurate is your understanding of your partner's picture of you.

A large amount of research has been conducted which points strongly to the view that love cannot be blind. The better each person understands the other's perceptions of himself and his world, the more satisfactory the relationship.

DEVELOPING THROUGH ONE ANOTHER

One of the main reasons for writing this book was to attempt to convince people that it is possible to grow, develop and change through their relationships instead of in spite of them. The following exercises are all designed to heighten one's sensitivity to oneself, one's partner and the world around one.

EXERCISE 1: *Pharaoh's Tomb*
Approximate time = any period

In the routine that is called daily living we tend not to see our partners clearly, but as afterimages of what used to be there. We talk and listen to a stereotype rather than to a changing human being. We develop stereotyped patterns of interaction where so much is predictable that spontaneity and novelty, when they exist, are not seen because we are wearing the wrong spectacles.

Similarly, we become habituated to the environments in which we live and work. This exercise has, as its objective, a renewed look at the world surrounding us, thus developing our sensitivity to objects, while simultaneously discovering new facets of our partner's personality.

The Egyptian Pharaohs had their tombs filled with mementos of their lives: toys from childhood, first and best-loved weapons, objects relating to significant events or periods. What would you choose to fill your tomb?

List the objects and then tell your partner.

What objects that surround you in your everyday living would you place in your tomb for no other reason than their aesthetic value?

EXERCISE 2: *"The Body Beautiful"*
Approximate time = thirty minutes

This exercise is aimed at increasing aesthetic sensitivity to your partner's body and to your own. Its title is taken from the early Charles Atlas advertisements in which one of the joys of

6. From their beautifully written book, *The Mirages of Marriage,* W. W. Norton, New York, 1968.

71

possessing a "body beautiful" was to be able to kick sand in the bully's face. Because of this the term is now used only for parody, and there is a general air of amusement surrounding the "better physique" movement. However, unlike that movement, we are not concerned with helping you to develop the biggest pectorals this side of the Atlantic. Just as we believe that we so easily miss out on meaningful and aesthetically pleasing experiences in the course of everyday life, so we believe also that many people are ashamed of their own bodies and get little pleasure from their partner's body, except as a fleeting prelude to sex. It is quite true that on looking around us we may see many good reasons for lack of pride in our physiques. This exercise is based on the notion that any physique will have something appealing about it. Awakening our sensitivity to this may lead to a resolution to make the rest of our body appealing, flexible and alive.

. . . Man is a biological organism. His first point of inhibition is in his physical structure . . . Bodily joy comes not simply from an athletic body but from one that functions smoothly, gracefully, without unnecessary strain; a body in which the joints move easily, the muscles are toned, the blood flows vigorously, the breathing is deep and full, food is digested well, the sexual apparatus is in good order, and the nervous system works effectively.
William C. Schutz[7]

---

1. Both people are naked. Each person has to say which part of his partner's body he finds most aesthetically pleasing, and why.
2. Ask your partner to give you complete control over that part of his body for you to do whatever you feel like doing. This has ranged from kissing to caressing, biting, cuddling and even eating food off it! One hot summer night a girl we know ate ice cream off her husband's thighs!

7. *Joy: Expanding Human Awareness,* Grove Press, New York, 1967.

EXERCISE 3: *Sticky Fingers*
Approximate time = time of eating a meal

The path from childhood to adulthood is lined with inhibitions. Many are necessary to enable us to participate in civilized society, but what is lost is the freedom to enjoy oneself totally in an activity in a way natural to a child.

This simple exercise is intended to recapture the innocence of childhood. Some people revel in it, others are just glad that they are inhibited. Society's ballast is too difficult to cast off.

The experience consists of eating a normal meal—but only using one's fingers. Notice how revolting it first feels to plunge your hand into your gravy or fried egg, then see how quickly it does not seem to matter any more. Try feeding one another. Be aware of the different textures and temperatures. Talk about it with one another.

EXERCISE 4: *Sharing Fantasies*
Approximate time = one hour

Caution: This exercise can be very powerful and sometimes people have experienced a hypnotic trancelike state from which they have found it difficult to emerge. If you have any reason to believe that you are the kind of person who is easy to hypnotize we would not advise you to perform this exercise. If your partner does get into a trance, you must talk him out very slowly, and with confidence.

We have been concerned up until now with heightening one's sensitivity to the outer world: *seeing* where you had previously only looked. Now it is time to discover more about the inner world, the realism of ambitions, fears, guilt, joys and potential for self-development.

It is helpful to first relax the body, using the relaxation procedure which you will have learned from the previous section.

One person helps the other to relax. When they are truly relaxed he says something which approximates to the following:

> "Close your eyes. I now want you to imagine that you are going to envelop yourself in a cocoon. This may be made of any material you like. Imagine what it would be like . . . cover yourself until you are warm and secure . . . what is it like inside there? . . . how do you feel? . . . what can you see? . . . what does it smell like?"

> (After a suitable period of time has elapsed, the "guide" continues:)

> "You are now going to become very small in your cocoon. It is getting larger and larger . . . it is now a whole world . . . and you are the only person in this world . . . what does it feel like? . . . and look like? Explore your world, see what you can find there."

> (After an appropriate time period, the guide continues:)

> "You may invite someone to join you in your world if you like, or you can choose to be alone."

> (The guide should now check as to whether someone is to be invited in. If this is the case, the fantasy continues:)

> "You can invite as many people into your world as you wish. Imagine what you would do together. What does it feel like to live in your world . . . sad, happy, colorful, calm, exciting?

> "The time has come now to leave your world and return to this world. How do you feel about that? You must bid good-by to all those in your world. . . . I'm going to count backward from five to one. When I reach one you will open your eyes, stretch like a cat waking up and sit up ready to talk."

The counting backward routine is a good one to repeat.

This exercise can provide a very moving experience, sometimes delightful, sometimes alarming. Some people find that emotive music in the background helps. Others like to describe their fantasies as they are happening. The best guide is simply to do what seems most natural to you.

Usually, people wish to discuss their fantasies afterward with their partner. This can be very illuminating. You should try to be particularly aware of what these fantasies say about you as a person.

A second fantasy experience is directed at discovering one's feelings about one's body. It is an attempt to replicate the journey central to the science fiction novel and film *The Fantastic Journey,* namely, into one's own body.

This is best done with one person asking questions and the "journeying" partner replying.

A real example will illustrate this:

Guide: "You may start your journey from any part of your body, John. Find your entrance."

John: "I am going up my nose. It is wet and dark. Like a swamp. Ugh! It's really revolting . . . like a great sewer, and liquid is dripping on me."

(John had a hangup about blowing his nose in front of people and seeing mucous from his or anyone else's nose made him feel sick.)

"I have now managed to slither to the top of this passage. Above me I can see great jelly globules, all shimmering, with sparks flying from one to the other. I don't want to get tangled up with that lot, so I'll go south."

(He was describing the underside of his brain.)

"There is a big drop, and I have landed on an enormous sponge, which is constantly moving. The movement is making me feel sick. There are great tombstones all around me, some are decaying. This is not a friendly place either, and it's still all wet. There's a stream running along the bottom, which looks fresh and clean. I'll follow that. I am now near a deep hole. It's not dark and there are notches cut in the wall which I can climb down. I'm halfway down and on both sides of me are tunnels leading to great white bags. I peer inside. They are constantly heaving in and out, and inside I see wet, black muck sitting there. It is revolting. I have no desire to go down there. I continue and finally reach the bottom of the tube. I am standing by a sort of trap door, which is glistening and inviting."

(John loved food but was concerned about his health so regulated his diet. His well-regulated eating habits are reflected in the clean, well-ordered food passageway, and the fresh saliva stream. His disgust of smoking is apparent, and he is uncertain about his mouth, which has led to worries about his health.)

"I open the trap door and inside there is an aluminum-lined tank. Water washes all sides periodically. There is a ladder, which I climb down. On the floor there is another trap door—also clean and bright. I open it and I am met by a foul smell. I really don't want to go down there, but there's no other way. There's no ladder here, but the tunnel slopes gently and so one can walk or slide along. The surface is getting more slippery and the smell worse. Oh God! There are lumps of shit around. I'm having to climb over some because there's no way round it. God, it's awful. I wish I could get out of here. It seems to go on for miles. Ah! There's a passage to the right. The smell is less here, and it is clean. I'm having to climb upward now, and there's a lot of movement. It's difficult to keep my balance."

(John was a product of severe toilet training and had a horror of feces. The thought of getting some on his hands was enough to bring him out in a cold sweat. He felt easier about urine and is now climbing up what presumably is an erect penis.)

"There is a roaring sound behind me. A tidal wave, all foaming, is going to knock me off my feet. I'm being swept along by it. There is a loud pop as I am squeezed through a small hole, and suddenly all is calm. It's moist in here and dimly lit, but it's very warm and wherever I stand or lie it's comfortable. The floor molds itself to fit my body."

(John was now in his wife's vagina. It is a fairly unusual occurrence for someone to fantasize out of his own body into someone else's, but not unknown. Note how much happier he is in her body than he was in his own. There is no disgust, no dirt. Even the moisture is comforting instead of "slimy."

John had a very close relationship with his wife, who had many virtues that he admired but felt he did not possess. He was always happiest with her when they were physically close. She provided him an enormous security, which he needed.)

Guide: "What are you going to do now, John?"

John: "It is tempting just to stay here, but I feel that I should explore. I must not be lazy."

(John needed his wife as a symbol of security and was aware of the fact that sometimes he forgot to see her as a person.)

Guide: "What else can you find?"

John: "Nothing. There is no way up from here. I've searched and the only exit is the one I came from."

Guide: "How do you feel about that?"

John: "Very sad. I feel that I have been kept from some treasure. Where I am is beautiful, but I want more. I suppose I will have to come out."

In the ensuing discussion it became clear that John felt he could get no further because he was not wanted. He could always receive shelter, but real friendliness was missing. He did not know what was beyond the "womb."

This fantasy gave them both much to work on.

Caution: Beware of psychoanalyzing. Although one can obtain many useful cues about one's feelings and problems, this can be overdone.

EXERCISE 5: *A Musical Evening*
Approximate time = as long as you want

Each person is to arrange a program of music for an evening, or for part of an evening. This can be made up from a record or tape collection or from borrowing records from a library or from friends. The theme dictating choice should be music that means much to you—either because of its aesthetic appeal or its symbolic significance. Each piece of music should be introduced with an explanation for the choice and any particular parts to which the player wishes the listener to attend.

From this exercise one can learn more about one's partner, and possibly about styles of music to which one normally closes one's ears. Be open to new musical experiences. You will not like everything, but see if there might be something you are missing.

This same exercise can be conducted using poetry and/or prose-reading evenings, painting reproductions, evenings out, playing games, etc.

The hardest battle is to be nobody-but-yourself in a world, which is doing its best, night and day, to make you like everybody else.
e. e. cummings

4·Learn to Fight Effectively

*It is not a partner's sweet and loving side that shapes his bond
with an intimate; it is the talent for airing aggression that counts
most.*

George Bach and Peter Wyden[1]

Many people feel uncomfortable in the presence of high
tempers and low emotional control. Nasty things may be said,
and nasty things hurt people; so we do not say them. Instead
of hurting others we merely hurt ourselves by allowing the
vitriol to build up and poison mind and body—this is considered to be more culturally acceptable. The ways in which
people cope with conflict are determined by nationality, social
class and religion. The French sociologist Emile Durkheim[2]
suggested that in Roman Catholic countries people murder
each other, while in Protestant lands they commit suicide.
His argument was that Protestants are preoccupied with their
own responsibility for what happens in their lives. Catholics
are not encouraged to refer to their own consciences but to
the body of the Church. Consequently, if a Catholic commits
a sinful act he does not need to feel guilty because he simply
refers to the priest for guidance. The Protestant refers to his

1. *The Intimate Enemy, op. cit.*
2. J. A. Spaulding and G. Simpson (trans.), *Suicide: A Study in Sociology,* Free Press, New York, 1951.

own conscience in a personal communication with God and is racked with guilt. Hence, the Catholic directs his attention away from himself to a higher authority to which he is responsible. The Protestant holds himself personally responsible. Durkheim argued that in times of stress Protestants are more likely to blame themselves when things go wrong, while Catholics are more inclined to accuse others. Present-day folklore reflects these differences—the enraged Italian discovers his wife in bed with her lover and kills them both, while the Swede withdraws to a wooden hut on a lonely island to ponder the evil that men visit on other men, as he gazes into the stark beauty of a setting Baltic sun.

The Anglo-Saxon heritage from our Protestant past is summed up by the football morality of "may the best man win" and keep your upper lip stiff at all times.

The main result of this is that both at home and at work people in this culture have developed a nose for sniffing out conflict to enable them to retreat hastily from it. The traditional slogan is

---

CONFLICT IS DESTRUCTIVE
AND
A BAD THING

We intend to argue that

CONFLICT CAN BE CONSTRUCTIVE
AND
A GOOD THING

Why is it that people in our culture shy away from an open conflict?

1. It is embarrassing for the people involved, who feel uncomfortable.
2. It can hurt people's feelings.
3. It can destroy relationships.
4. It prevents people from working effectively together.
5. "It only makes things worse."

Conflict, undoubtedly, can do all of these things. But it can also be a tremendous aid to personal growth and to the development of a positive relationship between two people.

The Chinese word for *crisis* has two meanings: one denotes "danger," but the other signifies "opportunity."

Conflict energizes any situation, and the energy provides the wherewithal for construction or destruction. In a relationship where two people fight incessantly there is an emotional involvement, however perverse it may be. In a polite relationship, there is no energy, only apathy. The distance between love and hate is considerably shorter than that between love and indifference. Edward Albee in his play *Who's Afraid of Virginia Woolf?* describes a relationship which, however monstrous it appears to others and to themselves, pulses with energy. But living at the center of an emotional holocaust, George and Martha are always involved with each other— never indifferent. The question which they have never resolved is how to use this tremendous interpersonal energy without destroying each other.

Some couples feel that their relationship is strong only because of their incessant fighting, and if the boxing ring were superseded by the dovecote there would be nothing left to shake hands on. In these situations the tendency to run away from conflict suffers an equally ironical twist and people feel self-confident in the face of aggression and uncertain in the presence of harmony.

LOVE AND HATE ARE RELATED

Psychotherapists, marriage guidance counselors and trainers of sensitivity and encounter groups commonly report how people hurl vitriol and spit venom at, or about, their partners, and yet, at the end of it all, the kernel that remains is a feeling of love, not hate.

The positive cannot come out until the negative does also. This is why, in analysis, the negative is analyzed, with the hope . . . that the positive will then be able to come into its own.

Rollo May[3]

If a person feels aggressive toward his partner and he suppresses that aggression, then his love for that person may be suppressed also—one more example of how unspoken conflict can strangle love.

USING CONFLICT CONSTRUCTIVELY

Our message is that, if you fight, this book may help you to develop your relationship more easily than if you are both apathetic about it. Apathetic relationships can be regenerated but emotions have first to be reignited. A marriage like that depicted in *Who's Afraid of Virginia Woolf?* simply needs to learn how to control the fire that is already there so that it does not consume the couple in its ferocity. This is not to say that a marriage without conflict is a dead thing, only that

3. *Love and Will, op. cit.*

where conflict exists it might be used to make the relationship stronger and more satisfying. Conflicts can be categorized.

SUPPRESSED CONFLICTS

Many apples look fresh and healthy and it is not until they are dissected that the maggots are discovered. Suppressed conflict is maggotlike and similarly spreads through the entire body of the fruit until the surface also bears the marks of its ravaging. There are two varieties of suppressed conflict—one where both partners are aware of an issue and tacitly agree not to talk about it, and the other where one person is aware of a conflict but the other is not.

Joe and Lynne were both successful doctors. They had met as students, married just before graduating, and had jobs in the same group practice of general practitioners. Joe was very enthusiastic about children. Lynne had always said that she supposed she would want children one day, but that she wanted a few years in which to practice medicine. As the years went by, their combined incomes provided them with a very luxurious style of life. They were both highly involved in their jobs and thoroughly enjoyed working together. Joe knew that it would become increasingly difficult for Lynne to give up this life in return for motherhood. They had a strong and loving relationship which Joe was frightened of jeopardizing by trying to persuade Lynne to do something that she really had no desire to do. Lynne knew of Joe's love of children and felt increasingly guilty at her horror of motherhood, yet she knew that she would perpetually resent Joe if she was stuck at home with children while he went off each day to do the work which she enjoyed. So they never talked about it. And, as the years went by, Joe became more bitter and his bitterness was expressed in nagging about mistakes Lynne occasionally made at work. Lynne felt increasingly guilty and this expressed itself in her working longer hours to justify the usefulness of her work to Joe and to herself. This in turn irritated Joe, who complained that if she was more efficient in her job she would not have to spend so many extra hours working. Yet they were both afraid to discuss the real conflict which existed between them. Both felt it was so fundamental that it could destroy the marriage.

We have picked this case study quite deliberately because it expresses a genuine conflict of interests. Although many conflicts between individuals are a result of lack of trust, low self-confidence, poor communication and self-defeating ways of behaving, undoubtedly there are some conflicts which reflect a genuine difference of interest. Joe's longing for children and Lynne's refusal to have any is an example of a genuine conflict of interests. It can only be resolved by one of them agreeing to do something that they would not choose to do. But it is better to accept this situation and decide who is to give way, and how the other person can make it as easy and as face-saving a decision as possible, than to ignore the conflict which can spread like a cancer through the entire relationship. Joe and Lynne were fortunate in that they were able to resolve their conflict by something approaching a compromise rather than one person capitulating, although it took a marriage guidance counselor to help them through the legacy of bitterness their conflict had bequeathed to them. Because of their common occupation they agreed to establish a family unit more common in Scandinavia than this country and described graphically by Rhona and Robert Rapoport in their book *Dual Career Families*.[4] As Joe wanted a child and Lynne did not, he agreed to merge their domestic and work roles. Their two jobs were transformed into one job in the practice. Joe would look after their child three days a week and Lynne for the other two days, as neither would accept someone else looking after their child.

4. Published by Penguin Books Ltd., Harmondsworth, 1971.

Another example of suppressed conflict involved Robert and Linda, but this time it was a conflict of which only Robert was aware.

Linda had never been very enthusiastic about sex with Robert, the main reason being that she had never had great sexual expectations. Consequently, Robert always had to initiate sex, and felt sick of appearing to be the only one with a sexual appetite. He felt as if he were always being caught with his fingers in the cookie jar while Linda was lucky enough to have been born without a sweet tooth. Robert had always been tolerant of this gray factor in an otherwise colorful married life and so Linda was unaware of his resentment. She only knew that something was wrong when Robert began to be uncharacteristically critical about her in many small ways.

What both of these case studies show about suppressed conflict is that the harder one or both partners has to work at suppressing the problem, the more likely his behavior is to become destructive in other ways.

"I HEAR MUSIC AND MY FEET BEGIN TO TAP" CONFLICTS

John was a moderately successful advertising account executive. He felt that he could be much more successful if he had more support from his wife, Patricia. They had two children, whom Patricia loved dearly, but she found the roles of wife and mother lacking something vital to her existence. She envied John his freedom and the range of stimulating people and problems that he met each day. Because of her boredom and frustration John felt an obligation to be at home as much as possible. He felt this prevented him from much social mixing in the evenings which might have furthered his career. So he resented Patricia for forcing him to feel guilty about her position as mother of his children.

A range of solutions are available to deal with this particular conflict, or rather series of conflicts—housewife versus career woman, job advancement versus domestic responsibility, husband's expectations of a wife's role versus her expectations of a wife's role, wife's expectations of a husband's role versus husband's expectations of that role. However, a workable solution was not arrived at prior to marital counseling. The reason—a stereotyped communication pattern which neither could break. We have used an example of John and Patricia's communication pattern to open this book (p. 11). We give what each says to the other (the "text") and what is really meant by what is said (the "subtext"). From this example it is quite clear that neither John nor Patricia is really listening to what the other is saying, and in particular to the underlying subtext. They are performing a set piece in which the scripts have been written some time before the performance. John says ABC and Patricia responds predictably with DEF, to which John answers GHI and so on *ad nauseam*. As soon as the music begins to play they cannot help their feet tapping in time to it. The natural rhythm takes control and the conflict tango begins again.

Many of the exercises in this book have been designed to try to break this form of stereotyped communication pattern. The usual device is to allow one person to talk without interruption, and before answering, the partner must check that he has understood the subtext of what has been said. So many married couples spend long periods of time just not listening to one another. They expect to know what their partner is likely to say and answer on that basis instead of in terms of what their partner has actually said.[5]

5. The exercises in communication on pages 114–136 are all designed to help people listen to what their partner is saying.

MANUFACTURED CONFLICTS

One way of avoiding a genuine conflict is to confuse the issue with a superficial conflict. A conflict which is *not* threatening to the couple is manufactured to disguise the real conflict which *is* threatening. The case study of Joe and Lynne (discussed previously) is an example. They developed a conflict about Lynne spending too much time at work in order to disguise their real concern about having children.

TRANSPARENT CONFLICTS

This applies to a situation where two people understand all the issues involved. There is no concealment or manufactured hostility. Jack says to Jill this is what I really want and this is how I really feel. Jill understands just what Jack wants but feels that she cannot go along with it.

The other categories may not represent genuine conflicts. If people were open with one another they would realize that perhaps there is no real difference of interest at all. Transparent conflict is always real and as such provides the greatest challenge to a relationship. A couple have to compromise or one has to give way. There are no other alternatives except to end the relationship, which sometimes has to happen. Here are a number of questions to ask one another if you suspect that an open conflict exists:

1. What do I want and what does my partner want?
2. Are these mutually exclusive? (In other words, are our demands such that only one or the other of us can be satisfied at a time?)
3. What are the consequences for us if I let her need take priority over my need?
4. What are the consequences for us if my need takes priority over her need?
5. Is a compromise possible?

Let us follow through Mary and Ted's answers to these questions.

1. Ted wants Mary to stay at home and look after their first child. Mary wants to continue with her work and place the child in a day nursery.
2. These are mutually exclusive.
3. If Ted gives in, he will resent Mary for going to work and perceive her as neglecting their child. Mary will know this and feel guilty for neglecting her child, but will resent Ted for making her feel guilty, as she has guilt feelings to cope with anyway. Result: Ted will be unhappy, Mary will be unable to enjoy her work, and the child will suffer through living in a home with conflict.
4. If Mary gives in, she will resent Ted for having the freedom of going to work each day and will hate the monotony of her domestic life. Ted will feel guilty about Mary doing something that she does not want to do. Result: again, both will be dissatisfied.
5. Possible compromises: (a) not having a child—but both want children; (b) dual career structure—not practical and neither could accept this anyway; (c) part-time work for Mary and employing a woman to look after the child in his mother's absence—Mary cannot work part-time in her occupation (a buyer for a clothing firm) and she does not want any job just for the sake of it. Result: no compromise is possible.

The situation is now clear. If the relationship is to continue, one of them must give in. In their favor is the fact that they have worked out all the consequences and therefore know what they have to work on. The actual result was that Ted gave in because the effect of Mary's capitulation was likely to be a greater threat to the marriage. Ted knew that he must be supportive to Mary, who felt guilty about this anyway. Mary knew that when she was at home with the child she must give him all of her attention for everyone's sake. She decided never to go away on business that involved an overnight stay unless this was absolutely necessary. She managed to persuade her employer to allow her to leave work at four o'clock each day and she agreed that, if the child appeared to be suffering in any way, she would give up her job. But all of this was possible only because they had been honest with one another about their feelings. They were aware of the consequences for each of them following from all possible decisions. Above all, they did not simply *tolerate* the other's ambitions. This is vitally important.

TOLERATION ALONE CAN BE DESTRUCTIVE

Few people are saints. If they tolerate another person's foibles or ambitions for too long without getting some sort of return, resentment inevitably sets in. It is no good saying that this should not happen—it does. It is one of the facts of strife.

SELFISHNESS IS THE KEY TO MARITAL SUCCESS

A marriage has the best chance of satisfying the needs of both partners if each is absolutely open about what he or she wants from the relationship. We do not marry simply to love and cherish another human being. We marry someone because we want a friend or we are sexually aroused by them; we want marital status; we want a confidant, someone to depend on, or someone to depend on us. We do not like a cold bed at night or eating alone. We want children and security; we want a place to bring the boss home to or an excuse to leave our parents' home. We want emotional warmth or perhaps a more distant relationship. We wish to do everything together or go our separate ways. In short, we all want something from our partner and our partner wants something from us. If we are open about our selfish needs it is quite likely that many of both partners' needs can be satisfied by the marriage. If this is not possible and sacrifices have to be made, both must know who is making what sacrifices. This is where tolerance is a virtue. Sacrifices made when the sacrificer feels that his partner is unappreciative of what he is doing cause resentment.

The injunction to be unselfish is an impossible ideal. Each of us is totally selfish in the sense that we are always doing what some part of us wants to. Generosity feels at least as rewarding as greed. Selfishness is neither inherently good nor bad—it depends on the way we are selfish as to whether it nourishes or injures.

Hugh Prather[6]

SOLVING PROBLEMS TOGETHER

Some couples play the "therapist-patient" game. Jill discovers that Jack is having a number of affairs. She waits for a while before doing anything, but there is no change in Jack's behavior. She is afraid to confront him in case this signifies the beginning of the end of their marriage. Instead she consults friends and relatives, and eventually she sees a guidance counselor. This in itself is a constructive use of interpersonal resources. She decides not to confront Jack but instead to pretend she does not know of the situation, making herself

6. *Notes to Myself, op. cit.*

more sexually desirable, engineering social engagements to give him less free time and discovering as much as she can about his girl friend in order to understand where the attraction lies. In other words, Jack has a "problem," namely, that he fancies other women. Jill sets about "curing" this problem. If she succeeds, Jack will be "well" again and not want other women. As in the typical medical setting, the patient is manipulated by the therapist, who decides when he is ill and when he is cured. The notion of joint diagnosis and treatment is still a revolutionary approach in the world of medicine, if not in theory then certainly in practice. Similarly, husbands and wives are often tempted to try to solve their partner's problem *for* them instead of *with* them. To confront anyone with a highly emotionally charged subject is risky, but often, where the risks are highest, the potential payoff can be greatest. Not to take risks in our personal relationships may be at best a guarantee of gray mediocrity, and at worst a gradual deterioration into a zombie marriage.

A zombie marriage is that depressingly well-known domestic scene of two colorless figures, shadows of their former selves, separate in their own dead worlds in mutually excluded orbits, who, when they do by accident collide, cause not a novalike explosion but a dusty thud. The path of the no-risk relationship can rapidly deposit you in this universe of the ice-pack wife, the impotent droop and the flaccid bedsprings.

The surest way of staving off zombiedom is to remember the maxim

---

NO RECONCILIATION WITHOUT CONFRONTATION[7]

---

7. We are indebted to Michael Jones for this slogan, which he generated during a group dynamics workshop conducted by Barrie Hopson.

When differences of opinion arise, emotions dominate reason, impulsiveness takes over from guardedness and people are hurt.

The alternatives are twofold: (a) to pretend that the episode never occurred; (b) to accept that it has happened and learn from the experience.

Pretending that it has never happened can lead to a reconciliation by mutual collusion, but too often the odor lingers on and emotional deodorants are not yet marketed. If two people force themselves to talk about their relationship, they may create opportunities for a new, deeper level of understanding and mutual coexistence. "Kiss and make up" too often leads to "kiss and rake up" when future quarrels occur. Instead, try following a policy of "kiss and shake up"—shake up and loosen the ways in which you behave toward one another, and develop new styles of interacting.

Our marriage used to suffer from arguments that were too short. Now we argue long enough to find out what the argument is about.

Hugh Prather

The well-known psychologist Kurt Lewin describes the process of change within a person or group of people as moving through the process of:

FREEZING—UNFREEZING—FREEZING

We all have a characteristic set of behaviors and attitudes which are frozen within us. We cannot hope to change unless we can unfreeze all of these before refreezing into a rather different form.

This book is concerned with helping people to thaw out

their behaviors and attitudes toward their partners in order to enable them to see what is appropriate and what is not. Human relationships should ideally consist of a constant process of unfreezing and freezing. One of the dangers of the "therapist-patient" game is the assumption that once *the* problem has been solved, all will be well. Life is not like this. People and situations are constantly changing, albeit at differing rates. Nothing stays the same. One problem solved triggers off numerous others. This is why it is important in a relationship not just to solve a problem but to discover a style for solving problems. This is where the "therapist-patient" model usually breaks down, because one person has sole responsibility for problem solving and he usually collapses under the strain, leaving a confused partner wondering just what has been happening around him.

One victim of this pattern was Brian. He left school at sixteen and ten years later was a moderately successful sales representative. He married Pamela, a graduate in English, to whom he felt intellectually inferior. He could not enter into discussions with Pamela and her friends, but felt that there was something of value in literature and drama from which he was excluded. This led Brian to refuse to visit Pamela's friends or to stay at home when they visited her. The situation reached a crisis point when Brian did not come home one night and Pamela discovered that he had spent the night with a girl who worked in one of the stores he called on. Although terribly hurt and angry, she realized after a violent confrontation with Brian that this was his way of hitting back at what he perceived to be her intellectual supremacy. He had consciously chosen a girl who was his intellectual inferior and who made him feel masculine for the first time for many months. The outcome was that Brian began to attend university extension classes in English literature. He enjoyed this enormously, and a potential marriage-breaking problem was resolved. However, Pamela was a teacher in a community school, which necessitated her being at the school for two evenings a week. Brian had two classes on different evenings and regular trips to theaters and films on weekends. Consequently, a new problem was born; they now did not see enough of one another, and Pamela in particular was irritated by this. Their eventual solution was to start a family, at which point Pamela gave up teaching. By the time the child was born, Brian was studying for a degree in English and history, which took up many of his evenings. Pamela resented this because after a fairly unstimulating day she expected her husband's company at night . . . and . . . *ad infinitum.*

There is nothing depressing about this. Life is concerned with the definition of "NOW" problems, some pleasant, some unpleasant, which have to be resolved.

The rainbow is more beautiful than the pot at the end of it, because the rainbow is now. And the pot never turns out to be quite what I expected.

Hugh Prather

Each new experience a relationship faces offers an opportunity for the two people involved to extend themselves. We can all learn from experience but some people need to go to evening classes.

EXPLORATION NOT CONDEMNATION

This is the way toward growth. Condemnation simply signifies that we are still unable to thaw out. Loosen up and learn.

Change can be the lifeblood of a marriage. Personal change can mean that instead of changing partners one can still have a never-ending source of variety which is easier on the bank balance and less wearing on the psyche. To elaborate on Edmund Burke, "a state without the means of some change is without the means of its conservation." This is as true for the married state as for the political state.

However, if change is the builder of satisfying marriages, humor is its bricks and mortar. One is aware in writing any book on marriage that it is only too easy to paint a picture of two intense souls living in a slush of togetherness while examining in the minutest detail the fluff in each other's navels.

The overall aim of this book is to generate joy. We believe everyone has the potential to find joy in himself and others, and to generate joy in mutual exploration of the range of experiences life has to offer. Sadly, too many people forget how to be joyful in the uninhibited ways of their childhood. Joy is a delicate flower that is only too vulnerable to the cold climates that many couples generate for their existence.

HOW TO GENERATE CHANGE

If you are dissatisfied with some aspect of your own life or of your marital relationship, how easy is it to change your situation?

Bill wants to change his job because he is unhappy with his present firm. This will almost certainly mean moving to another part of the country. He knows that Diana, his wife, will be very unhappy about this. How then does he attempt to create conditions which will render Diana more open to change? A typical approach used by many is to extol the virtues of the new job, the possibility of a beautiful new house, the opportunities of meeting new friends, a general broadening of horizons. However, using this approach is more likely to increase resistance to any move than to inspire Diana to uproot herself.

We can more easily understand how Diana's resistance is increased by using a very simple model developed by Kurt Lewin to demonstrate efficient and inefficient ways of achieving changes.

The pressures operating for and against the acceptance of change

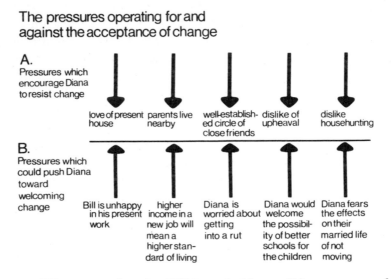

A.
Pressures which encourage Diana to resist change

love of present house | parents live nearby | well-established circle of close friends | dislike of upheaval | dislike househunting

B.
Pressures which could push Diana toward welcoming change

Bill is unhappy in his present work | higher income in a new job will mean a higher standard of living | Diana is worried about getting into a rut | Diana would welcome the possibility of better schools for the children | Diana fears the effects on their married life of not moving

The approaches that Bill has tried have all been concerned with reinforcing the upward pressures, namely, emphasizing the beneficial effects a move could have for him, their marriage, their standard of living and, consequently, their children.

However, our model is something of a physical one, and every physicist knows that if the forces operating on an object in a state of equilibrium are increased in one direction, then the forces in the opposite direction must increase equally if the equilibrium is to be maintained. This means that our arrows now look like this:

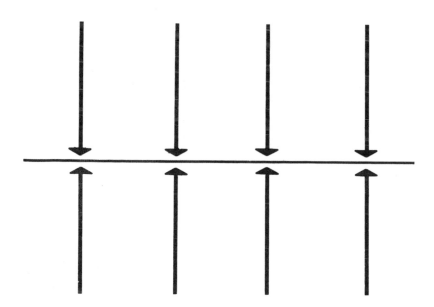

What has happened is that the forces operating on each side are now significantly stronger, and *tension* is at a higher level.

Diana's frustration will increase, and her resistance is likely to harden. This approach to generating change can be called *overcoming resistance*. It could be likened to trying to stop a car by using the brakes without taking one's foot off the accelerator.

What happens if Bill uses the other alternative open to him and concentrates on the downward forces (A) that make Diana resistant to change? This approach is called *reducing resistance*. If Bill tackles her concerns about moving and succeeds in reducing her resistance, then a new equilibrium is reached, but at a lower level of tension.

This is like stopping a car by taking one's foot off the accelerator, without using the brake.

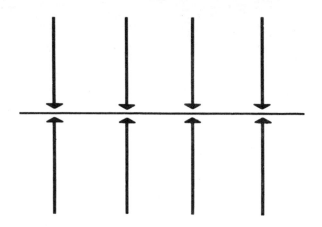

Using techniques like this may smack of manipulation. This is harsh. If one or both individuals desire change, then they want to maximize their chances of obtaining what they want.

MASTERMINDING

One must avoid the technique of "masterminding." In Bill's case, he would be guilty of this if he were to logically and coherently argue his case, and at each step in the argument Diana would be asked if she followed and would probably accept the point made. Because of his logical skill, Diana will find nothing wrong and will be forced to agree hesitantly. By the end of the discussion Diana would discover that she has agreed to the move because she has been "outargued" or masterminded at each stage in the process. Result: Bill leaves the discussion happy because he has convinced Diana of the advantages of moving; Diana leaves the discussion in agreement but uneasy, and a short time later the truth hits her yet again, "To hell with it, I really don't want to move." In addition, she is now resentful of Bill for having, as she sees it, manipulated her. It is no good for Bill to protest his innocence. Her perception is genuine. He must endeavor to see how she formed that impression.

MAKING DECISIONS TOGETHER

To be or not to be:
that is the question.
Whether 'tis nobler in the mind to
suffer the slings and arrows of outrageous fortune,
Or to take arms against a sea of troubles,
and by opposing end them.

Hamlet was faced with a dilemma which regularly confronts us all. Not whether to kill our mother's lover, but when put into a situation where a choice has to be made, whether or not to choose to act. A number of American psychologists have recently carried out work which suggests that people can be placed on a continuum. At one end are those who feel that they control their lives and, with obvious environmental limitations, are masters of their own destinies. Cassius in *Julius Caesar* was such a man:

Men at some time are masters of their fates:
The fault, dear Brutus, is not in our stars,
But in ourselves, that we are underlings.

At the opposing end of the continuum are those who feel that their fates are in the hands of more powerful forces, whether they be powerful people, political bodies, social and economic processes, or the supernatural. Listen to Guildenstern from Tom Stoppard's play *Rosencrantz and Guildenstern Are Dead:*

Wheels have been set in motion, and they have their own pace, to which we are . . . condemned. Each move is dictated by the previous one—that is the meaning of order. If we start being arbitrary it'll just be a shambles: at least, let us hope so. Because if we happened, just happened to discover, or even suspect, that our spontaneity was part of their order, we'd know that we were lost.

The terms we use to distinguish between these two opposing outlooks on life are:

PROACTIVE and REACTIVE

The basic difference is that a *proactive person* tends to make things happen *FOR* him, whereas a *reactive person* allows things to happen *TO* him.

In our experience, reactive people tend to gain less from life. They see themselves as pieces of human flotsam and jetsam tossed upon the sea of life with no control over their destiny. They are met in all walks of life:

> *Managing Director:* "I know profits are falling but I'm sure that things will right themselves next year."
>
> *Unemployed:* "Someday, something will turn up, if I'm patient."
>
> *Father:* "My boy's all right. He's not really a thief. He'll grow out of it."
>
> *Wife:* "I'm sure he'll give her up soon. I don't know what he sees in her."
>
> *Student:* "I've gotten through exams before. I don't suppose this time will be any different."

We have met numerous couples who feel that they have no freedom of action as far as their marriage is concerned.

> "He's always been like this. He'll never change now. There's nothing I can do."
>
> "I wish we could have a better sex life, but I suppose I've

just got to resign myself to the fact that he's just not that way inclined."

Year after year people continue to accept second-best—or worse—and feel powerless. Yet in a relationship between two people, both have power, perhaps in different proportions, but they have it nonetheless. If a man is uninterested in sex, it is his wife who allows him to remain uninterested. If a woman constantly nags, it is her husband who conspires with her to allow this to continue. Often, to break these habitual behavior patterns demands taking a real risk, which, in theory, could mean the end of the marriage. However, we feel that this will rarely happen in practice and, moreover, that marital breakdown in itself is not always negative. Sometimes separation is necessary in order to liberate both people so that they can find satisfaction and grow individually in a way that was not possible for them as a couple.

If you feel you are powerless, try drawing your own diagram (in the way we have just illustrated) showing the forces preventing you from changing your situation and in particular the forces that are operating in favor of change. The final chapter in this book is designed to help people to generate changes in their marital relationship.

TO MAKE A DECISION OR TO AVOID IT?

A satisfactory or unsatisfactory marriage does not simply "happen." The two people concerned are ultimately responsible for the kind of marriage they have. A whole series of decisions will have been made, many of them unconsciously, which will determine what the product looks like from outside, and what it feels like from within. He decides to get up first most mornings and make breakfast—she lets him. She decides to cook all the evening meals—he agrees without a word passing between them. He decides he wants to go out with the boys two nights a week—she does not agree. He decides to go anyway, and she does not try any harder to stop him.

Whether the relationship is satisfying or stultifying, decisions are continually being made—or avoided. Faced with the choice of whether to confront an unfaithful husband or leave him, a woman may persistently postpone making a positive decision. Making decisions is similar to making love. Most people assume that the skill comes naturally, but the divorce courts and the too numerous "together-but-lonely" people are evidence that it is an art that comes only with knowledge and practice. Fortunately, the market is well supplied with manuals on the techniques of making love, but there is little available to help people to make decisions.

PROACTIVE DECISION MAKING

The most effective decision making emanates from a person with a proactive outlook on life. He is more likely to possess the necessary resolve to make a decision than a reactive person, who simply hopes that "something will turn up" or waits for others to make decisions for him. The reactive person will always be able to blame others, or society, or the government when things go wrong, but he will never experience the joy of personal achievement and the feeling of being in control of his destiny.

However, having the resolve to make decisions is not enough; one must also have a strategy. We have found the following strategy to be a useful one:

1. *Define the problem or situation.* Many people run into difficulties because they never really define their problem clearly. Joan was unhappy living with Peter but she did not know exactly why this was. He was kind, helpful at home, loved her and the children, was apparently faithful,

and yet she was unhappy. She continued in this state until she was able to talk it through with a counselor, who helped her to discover that the cause was Peter's joylessness —his lack of intensity of mood. No matter what she did, he remained more or less contented but was never excited. She was a more volatile person and felt dampened by his presence. He defused every situation that she was ready to put a match to. Knowing the problem she could then work on it, difficult though it was.

2. *Collect all data relevant to the problem.* Joan had to be fully aware of her attitudes and Peter's attitudes, and to observe carefully for a few weeks to discover if Peter always acted like a dead weight or if he showed joy on any occasion.

3. *Define the alternatives.* Joan concluded that she could: (a) adjust to living with Peter as he was; (b) confront Peter calmly and share her concerns to see if together they could come to a solution; (c) try to change Peter by reinforcing his behavior whenever he did show joy; or (d) opt out of the challenge by leaving him.

4. *Define the implications of choosing each alternative.* Joan loved Peter and did not want to leave him, but she could not tolerate life as it was. The difficulty in reinforcing his behavior when he did show excitement was that this was only during football games and certain comedy shows on television. However, this did show that he was capable of spontaneous joy.

The only alternative was confrontation. Leonard Levinson defines aggression as "invading the issue." This is a more appropriate definition of confrontation. However, having decided to confront, there are more or less constructive ways of doing it: talk calmly, without blaming the other person—simply describe the situation, but simultaneously reassure him of your strong feelings towards him.

5. *Make the decision.* One of the alternatives must be chosen.

6. *Accept responsibility for the decision.* Joan was aware of the risks that she was running and knew that she would be responsible for the outcome, whether satisfactory or not.

7. *Implement the decision.* Joan confronted Peter. He was very upset, but Joan refused to let herself be caught up in a quarrel. She did not rise to the abuse which Peter hurled at her, realizing that his response was natural for someone facing a challenging personal criticism. They talked about the reasons for his lack of joy and spontaneity. This appeared to be rooted in his childhood, where no one in his family ever seemed to get excited over anything. The approach to life was downbeat. No one made a fuss over birthdays, Christmas, etc., and Peter never developed the capacity for behaving in a joyful manner. Joan suggested he try laughing out aloud. He could not do this. She then tickled him, and kept tickling him until he was rolling around the floor laughing helplessly. It was as if the barricades from years of restraint had been smashed down in one go. They discovered that he often did feel joy but never expressed it. He instructed Joan to tell him whenever he was talking in a monotonous voice, or dampening her mood, when by all accounts he should be excited. He resolved to try to introduce some spontaneity into their lives. He would occasionally arrive home with a present for Joan or the children when there was no special occasion. He would suddenly announce that they were going out for a meal that week or offer to prepare a weekend lunch. He occasionally wrote Joan a letter. This was for her the best thing of all.

8. *Evaluate the decision.* A few months after the confrontation with Peter, the improvement in the marriage was so apparent that Joan knew she had made the right decision. If it had not been the correct one she would have had to return to step (1) and begin the entire process again. By

taking a risk, by being proactive, and by adopting a constructive decision-making strategy, Joan had effected an improvement in her marriage that she wanted and had helped Peter to develop in a way that he wanted.

PROACTIVE DECISION AVOIDANCE

It is tempting to think that to avoid making a decision is probably always an inferior strategy to making one. This is misleading. There is a strategy of proactive decision *avoidance*. This is identical to proactive decision-making until it comes to (5) —making a decision. The decision is made to *avoid* making a decision. This is not a reactive step as there will be a good reason for doing it. Professor Alec Rodger coined the term "planned procrastination" referring to, for example, the process of choosing a career. If a student graduates from high school and no career appeals to him, it is sensible to delay his decision making until he has a clearer idea of what he wants, or until he obtains further qualifications, or until more information is available to him about himself and the world of work. This is more than just "procrastination." There is a purpose, a plan behind his decision to avoid making a decision.

Occasions will occur in married life when it will be sensible to do nothing for a certain time. If you suspect that your wife is having an affair, it might be best to delay any action until more evidence is available. When the evidence is overwhelming and you cannot bring yourself to confront your partner, that is when *planned procrastination* becomes merely procrastination—putting off the moment of choice. Of course, one decision you might make in that situation is not to confront, because you can accept adultery. That is not being reactive. It is only reactive behavior when you are unhappy in a situation and do nothing to improve it.

Sometimes one can avoid making a choice between two or more alternatives by choosing to do both in succession. This is called a *sequential strategy*.

Frank and Anne could not agree on which of two films to see. They avoided having to make a decision by going to see them both on different evenings.

Another proactive decision-avoiding strategy is the *omnibus strategy*. This is where two or more alternatives can be achieved simultaneously.

George could not decide whether to become an accountant or a French language translator. He avoided having to choose between his two interests by beginning his accountancy training and continuing with his French studies in the evenings, in the hope that he might eventually become an accountant working for a continental branch of his firm, where his knowledge of French would be invaluable.

Someone once said that silence is not always golden. Sometimes it is just plain yellow. To suffer a lack of joy in one's life is to abdicate from one's responsibility to oneself, to one's partner and to life. Every person needs to grow, to develop and to change. It is possible to use the experience of married life, including its conflicts and confrontations, to achieve this. Grow, develop and change through your relationship instead of in spite of it. If this is not possible, then you have outgrown the relationship—nevertheless, this is preferable to the relationship outgrowing you.

5·Communication Is the Aim of the Game

Human existence is exemplified by one person trying to communicate with others. The complex nature of our societies is due in no small part to the sophisticated set of verbal and nonverbal symbols by which one person can convey his thoughts and feelings to another. However, just as our outstanding successes as social groups and as individuals result from our ability and inclination to communicate, so do our social and personal disasters. Words can be used to conceal as well as to convey truths. Even when we are sincere in our efforts to communicate, misunderstandings arise, so much so that there is a growing army of people whose job it is to sort out ambiguous communications and to train people to communicate more effectively.

Let us examine the communication process more closely.

The woman in our illustration, in attempting to communicate something to the man, has obviously failed to do so effectively. The result is that, somewhere between transmission and reception, the message has been distorted. This distortion is very common, and sometimes it is so great that the listener picks up the exact opposite of what the talker intended to communicate. What goes wrong?

Communication between two people depends on both verbal and nonverbal factors. Psychologists use the term "verbal communication" to refer only to the words that are spoken.

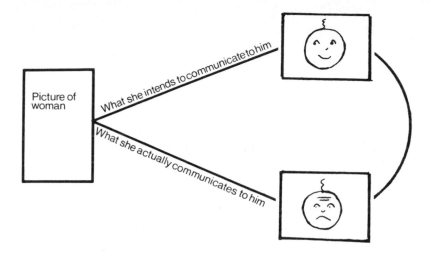

"Nonverbal communication" refers to the way in which they are spoken—tone, accent, pitch, hesitations; the way the person is looking—facial gestures and eye contact; the way he appears generally—posture, hand movements, clothes and physical appearance. All of these nonverbal factors will influence how a message is received. Psychological research has shown that when two people communicate, 93 percent of the total impact is transmitted nonverbally, and only 7 percent by the words that are used. Yet we have been taught to think carefully about the *words* we use, not the *way* we say them and the way we *look* when we are saying them.

"Come here, darling," can be said warmly, threateningly, seductively, authoritatively or pleadingly. It may be said accompanied by meaningful eye contact or no eye contact. The eye contact may register warmth or anger. Problems arise when the words and tone convey one message—warmth, for example—but the eyes and face convey anger. The message may be understood differently if the talker is fully dressed compared to being half-dressed!

Perfect communication will occur only if the listener sees

and hears all the channels in unison. This means that the words have to sound right and fit in with the situation and the speaker's manner, facial movements, posture and appearance. It is not surprising that distortion often takes place. Of course, the existence of nonverbal factors means that often a message can be conveyed very effectively without any words being used. In fact, research has shown that, out of the two—verbal and nonverbal factors—we tend to place more trust in the latter. The reason is simple: it is all too easy to deceive with words, whereas we are usually unaware of the nonverbal messages which we communicate. We are suspicious of people who communicate little nonverbally: "he has a poker face," "he's difficult to read." We feel uncomfortable in the presence of someone who wears dark glasses: this is because an important medium of nonverbal communication is blocked, and in addition, he is able to read our eyes. Result: we feel at a disadvantage.

Faulty communication is one of the major causes of breakdown in otherwise workable marriages. A wife has been working hard all day and looks forward to going to bed. However, once in bed the husband, feeling amorous, begins to caress her. She yawns significantly, closes her eyes and turns over. Her message is: "I am very tired after a hard day and I am desperate to get to sleep." What he hears is: "I don't want to make love to you." The implication for him is that he is being rejected, although that was not her intention.

Words can mean that I want to make you into a friend and silence can mean that I accept your already being one.

Hugh Prather

Except when they are asleep, whenever two people are living together they are communicating—through words, through silences, a kiss, buying a present, slamming a door, crying, sitting staring into space, cooking a favorite meal, playing with the children. In relating to another person it is impossible *not* to communicate. We have demonstrated how difficult it is to guess what another person is trying to say—all one can do is closely observe his behavior. The handshake is an illustration of this. Our forebears could not read each other's intentions but they could test to see if the sword hand was empty by shaking each other's right hand, the right hand being that in which the sword was usually carried.

People from different backgrounds have great difficulty in communicating with one another. This becomes clearest at an international level. There is an enormous difference between countries as to how much people touch one another. Englishmen are often horrified when talking to someone from the Middle East, who will stand much closer to him when talking as well as touching his arms, hands, and legs if sitting down. Jourard[1] counted the frequency of physical contacts per hour of couples in cafes in cities in different countries and found 180 in San Juan (Puerto Rico), 110 in Paris, 2 in Gainesville (Florida), and none in London. When visiting someone in West Africa in order to ask a favor it is assumed that a gift will be presented—not as a bribe, but as part of a tradition. Visitors to the United States will have to learn what happens at a barbecue, a baby shower and a bull session and may have to learn the elaborate rules which surround dating.

Unless one understands the nuances of meaning which accompany different behaviors and words, then distortion of communication is inevitable. This can happen within any society as well as between societies. People who marry from different social backgrounds will have a whole series of expectations about how their spouse should behave.[2] A middle-

1. "An Exploratory Study of Body-Accessibility," *British Journal of Social and Clinical Psychology,* 46 (1966), 130–138.
2. The effects of these on a marriage is discussed in Chapter 8.

class girl married to a lower-middle-class boy who goes out with the boys two or three nights a week may see this as an act of rejection, unfaithfulness or indifference, or she may simply believe that her husband has a drinking problem. As far as he is concerned, he is behaving normally and communicating nothing more than that. Some years ago Nancy Mitford described the distinction between "U and non-U" speech, respectively upper-class and non-upper-class speech. Here, the words that one uses indicate a whole life style and thereby communicate a great deal about their users. U speech has much in common with lower-working-class speech; non-U speech is euphemistic and characterizes the lower-middle classes. If a British parent doesn't want his child to be like "those dreadful working-class people" he will be taught to say toilet, lounge, dessert. The upper-middle-class parent who does not wish his child to be like "those dreadful lower-middle-class people" will teach the use of lavatory, sitting room and pudding. The middle-classes value privacy. In an upper-working-class home anyone who leaves the one room where all the family are gathered will be questioned as to where he is going. There is no perceived need for privacy.

BEWARE THE DOUBLE BIND

A message is called a "double bind" message when there are two contradictory messages contained in it. She says, "Come here, my darling," but with venom in her voice. Do you go or don't you? He says, "Why do you have to do everything I tell you?" What is she to do? If she complies with his demand, she is doing as he tells her, but if she ignores it, she continues to behave as he does not like.

Common double binds are demands for behavior that can only be spontaneous: "You must love me"; "Be more spontaneous"; "I want you to respect me more." By being ordered to do any of these and by complying, you logically cannot feel genuine love, be spontaneous or naturally feel respect.

MORE VERBAL TRAPS

The way we use simple everyday words often distorts communication.

We

By using "we," we can confirm areas of agreement, *e.g.*, "We would like to start a family." However, we often use "we" to whitewash real differences between us. You might say, "I think we agree on that," knowing that you disagree but you want to put over your point of view. In writing this book, we frequently use the word "we." As only one of us is writing at one time, I am assuming that my co-writer agrees with me. Sometimes there is disagreement and then one of us will say, "You can't use 'we' here; you are only referring to yourself. I have no ownership of that idea and have no wish to be associated with it."

Notice how many of your friends in groups of people say, "We feel that . . . ," "We would like to . . . ," "We disagree with . . ." They are pretending to speak for the whole group when all they are saying is "I feel that," "I would like to," "I disagree with."

But

"But" is often used to cancel out the first part of a sentence. As soon as anyone says, "I like living with you, *but* . . . ," the "I like living with you" is quickly forgotten by the listener, who only hears the approaching criticism.

Why

Asking questions prefaced with "why" can often sound hostile, expressing implied criticism. "Why are you home early?" makes one feel that some sort of justification is necessary. Converting it into a statement—"You are home early"—is much less threatening. Better still, ask, *"How* are you home so early?" This asks for an explanation, not a justification.

Questions beginning with "how" or "what" are requests for information. As John O. Stevens[3] puts it: "When you ask 'Why' you only ask for endless explanations—the cause of the cause of the cause of the cause."

You

When someone begins a sentence with "you," this often makes the other person feel defensive. Something is about to be directed personally at *you.*

Most, if not all, "you" statements are really camouflaged "I" statements. "You are selfish" really means *"I* think that you are selfish." "You" statements make it easy to blame the other person, ignoring the responsibility of the accuser in the suggestion. "You should be more affectionate" sounds as if the whole world would agree on this "fact." "I wish that you were more affectionate" makes it clear that this statement is only made in the context of the relationship. This is more likely to be received as constructive criticism than the generalization "You should be more affectionate."

CAUTION
Do not harken back to the past when working on exercises concentrating on "here-and-now" patterns of communication. The surest way to prevent constructive communication is to embark on a game of "law courts." This well-known marital game consists of the counsel for the prosecution drawing up a list of previous crimes to be taken into consideration, and the counsel for the defense responding. As there is no judge present, the case can never be satisfactorily concluded.

---

3. *Awareness: Exploring, Experimenting, Experiencing,* Real People Press, Moab, Utah, 1971.

It is factors like these which cause a multitude of problems because people cannot communicate if the other person does not possess a similar verbal and nonverbal vocabulary.

We can learn to be better communicators and to overcome these difficulties. That is the objective of this chapter. We can learn to be better listeners by:

1. Not hearing what we expect to hear but what is really said.
2. Giving undivided attention.
3. Not thinking about our own answers instead of paying full attention.
4. Not listening for details rather than for the essential message.

We can learn to be better communicators by:

1. Organizing our thoughts before speaking.
2. Not including too many ideas which are often unrelated.
3. Answering points made by the previous speaker and therefore responding to what has been said.

The first exercises explore our communication patterns at the verbal level, while the later ones concentrate on what we can convey nonverbally.

EXERCISE 1: *"I Believe"*
Approximate time = unpredictable

Many couples who have been married for some time say that one of the disadvantages of marriage is that after many years together there is nothing new to learn about each other. If this is true, it is certainly a very sad state of affairs, as what they are saying is that they are not developing as individuals or as a couple. Some people undoubtedly do stagnate. This would be of little concern in itself if people were happy in their stagnation, but most are not, as human beings do appear to be driven by a desire for new experiences. There is comfort in living with what we know and this provides us with our essential security. But whether it is the Indian peasant farmer or the jet-set executive, some change is always sought before a man can feel alive. Even those who abhor "change" are usually commenting on their dislike of certain technological and social changes, rather than the way in which they are developing as people. We change from child to adolescent to adult to spouse to parent to grandparent. Along this dimension alone lies a host of new experiences to stimulate us and from which we can learn something about ourselves and about life.

When couples say that they have nothing new to learn about each other, this is due to stereotyped communication patterns, unless they really do not like one another and have no interest in their partner. "We talk about the children, our holiday plans, our relations, and about plans for the house," said one woman we talked to. People get into the habit of talking about certain subjects in a particular way. The danger in a permanent relationship is that this format becomes ritualized into one's daily living. However, a man and a woman will have attitudes toward, and beliefs about, the purposes of child rearing, their expectations about marriage, religion, politics, entertainment, cultural pastimes, creative activities, etc. It is often surprising to find out not how *much* we do know about our partner, but how *little* we know. This happens sometimes because one or both feel that there is a taboo against talking about some subjects, but much more often because in the dailiness of family life we are too preoccupied with the tasks of living to relate to one another other than in a stereotyped way.

This exercise is aimed at shedding some light into the "hidden area" of our self-concepts, to discover what we really think and believe about a variety of subjects.

Each partner in turn answers the questions or completes an

incomplete sentence which follows. After each statement the
other person may ask questions.

The "I Believe" Worksheet

Marriage
1. Marriage for me means . . .
2. The ideal husband is one who . . .
   (Remember that each partner answers all questions.)
3. The ideal wife is one who . . .
4. What should a husband be prepared to do in relation to
   housework and child rearing?
5. What should a wife be prepared to do in relation to housework and child rearing?
6. How should children be brought up?
7. The ideal child should be . . .
8. The best thing about our sex life is . . .
9. The worst thing about our sex life is . . .
10. I feel that adultery is . . .
11. My feelings about sex education for children are . . .
12. Do you think that women are less interested in sex than men?
13. Love is . . .

Work
14. What I like best about my work is . . .
15. What I like least about my work is . . .
16. Why do people work?

Personal Issues
17. I am afraid of . . .
18. I believe in . . .
19. I am ashamed of . . .
20. The emotion I find most difficult to control is . . .
21. When I feel depressed I . . .
22. A friend is . . .

23. In the next ten years I hope to . . .
24. The person I most resent is . . .
25. The person I know that I most admire is . . .
26. My greatest anxieties are . . .
27. My most frequent daydreams are . . .
28. My background is . . .
29. What are your feelings about your childhood?
30. My feelings about money are . . .

Social Issues
31. My feelings about homosexuality are . . .
32. I think abortion is . . .
33. The greatest social evil is . . .
34. What do I care and do for my fellow men?
35. Do you approve of divorce?
36. I think that black people are . . .
37. Do you believe in premarital sexual intercourse?
38. Pornography is . . .
39. Violent criminals should . . .
40. Do you believe in the death penalty?
41. Should people be free to take their own lives?
42. I think honesty at all costs is . . .
43. Blood sports are . . .
44. Politicians are . . .
45. The politician I respect most is . . .
46. Should people demonstrate against the government?
47. The worker's right to strike is . . .
48. Do you believe that a person should always support his country?
49. Pacifists are . . .
50. Competition is . . .

Religion
51. Religious people are . . .
52. Do you believe in an afterlife?

53. Does religion enter at all into your daily life?
54. Should children be brought up with some religious beliefs?
55. God is . . .

Interests
56. I enjoy . . .
57. I cannot understand people who like . . .
58. What are your tastes in music?
59. To me art is . . .
60. I enjoy reading . . .
61. I like to watch . . .
62. My ideal film would be about . . .
63. My ideal evening on television would consist of . . .
64. Do you think that men and women are interested in different things?
65. At the theater I enjoy . . .
66. I would like to spend more time . . .
67. It would please me if you were interested in . . .
68. I would like to develop an interest in . . .
69. What have you discovered about me that is new?
70. Which new information about me has pleased you most?

There is probably nothing like living together for blinding people to each other.

Ivy Compton-Burnett

EXERCISE 2: *Acknowledge My Existence*[4]
Approximate time = one evening

One of the most commonly quoted complaints which spouses make against one another is that their partner does not listen to

4. This exercise is adapted from Lederer and Jackson's *The Mirages of Marriage, op. cit.*

them. People hear what they expect to hear and consequently do not listen. Many times each day someone says something to his spouse which is ignored, or acknowledged by a grunt or a nod of the head.

Jack: "God, what an awful day."
Jill: No comment.

Jill: "I made love passionately to the milkman this morning, dear. I couldn't resist him any longer."
Jack: "Really, that's nice."

A complete unit of communication consists of

1. Statement from first speaker.
2. Acknowledgment from listener that he has heard and understood.
3. Acknowledgment by the original speaker that he heard the acknowledgment.

A couple should attempt to spend an evening rigidly following this rule. At times you may feel silly, but what you will learn is just how little you do acknowledge one another's attempts to communicate, and thereby, at that instant, negate your partner's existence.
Examples:

Jill: "I hope you enjoyed your meal." (original statement)
Jack: "I enjoyed it very much." (acknowledgment)
Jill: "I'm glad you enjoyed it." (acknowledgment of the acknowledgment)

Jack: "I enjoyed that."
Jill: "Enjoyed what?"
Jack: "That play on television."

Jill: "You do annoy me."
Jack: "Why do I annoy you?"
Jill: "You just bury your head in that newspaper as soon as you come home."
Jack: "I'm sorry, it's just that I feel too tired to talk."
Jill: "You're always too tired."
Jack: "Yes, I'm afraid I am."

In this exchange, breaking off typically occurs between any pair of statements. Here it must continue as long as either person wishes it to do so.

At the beginning of this exercise the routine will often be forgotten. You must help each other to remember. If Jill says something which Jack fails to acknowledge, whether by grunting or no comment, Jill must say in a friendly manner, "Jack, are you going to acknowledge?" If Jack has acknowledged and Jill simply nods her head, Jack must politely remind Jill that she has to acknowledge his acknowledgment.

At the end of an evening, talk over what you have learned about the way you normally communicate with one another. See if there is anything that you can do which may permanently improve communications.

Some couples extend this exercise to a week or even longer until they are satisfied with the level reached.

EXERCISE 3: *Examine My Subtext*
Approximate time = flexible

Marshall McLuhan says that the medium is the message. Nowhere is this more appropriate than when two people are trying to communicate. The message that comes across is determined almost entirely by the person (medium) from whom it emanates.

Earlier, we gave an example of two people talking, and pointed out the difference between what is said (the text), and what underlies what is said (the subtext). This exercise is designed to make you sensitive to the subtext beneath your partner's words.

1. For one evening, morning or any convenient time period of at least two hours, both partners agree to carry on their normal living, but with the addition of one rule: always say what you think the subtext is behind what your partner says.

    There will not be any particular subtext accompanying everything your partner says. However, if you are aware that you meant something other than what you have said, and your partner has not picked up the subtext, you must take the initiative and explain your own subtext.

2. At the end of the designated time period, discuss what you have learned about the frequency of subtext used by one another and what you have discovered about each other.

EXERCISE 4: *Echo*
Approximate time = fifteen minutes

This is designed to demonstrate just how difficult it is to really listen to what someone says.

1. Both partners agree to talk about a particular topic. It is best if this is a subject which has some significance for them, for example, changing homes, a new job, starting a family, etc.

2. Jill opens the conversation. After she has said what she wants to say, before Jack can respond he has to repeat the essence of what Jill has said. If Jill is happy that Jack has really heard all the points, then Jack is free to respond. Similarly, Jill has to repeat what Jack says to her. Continue with this for about fifteen to twenty minutes. To begin with, conversation will appear disjointed, but people quickly get the hang of the procedure.

3. Discuss the difficulties of listening to one another. Some points

which might arise are: (a) Is there any difference in our listening ability depending upon whether we agree or disagree on a point? (b) How often do we not hear because we are thinking of the next thing we want to say? (c) Do we tend to use a new word or phrase when we repeat what we have heard which puts our own slant on the topic, *e.g.*

> Jill: "If we did move, there might be more room for the kids to play."
>
> Jack: *"One of the advantages* of moving would be that
> (repeating) the children *will* have more room to play."

Although the difference is subtle, it is clear that Jack is more in favor of moving than Jill is. The italicized words are those that give the repeat the more positive sounds than Jill's version. (d) How far do we take note of nonverbal cues, and which ones?

EXERCISE 5: *Reversal*
Approximate time = two to three hours

To see ourselves as our partner sees us is the aim of this exercise. It should shed light into that "bad breath" zone—the blind area of the self.

1. Put aside a time period of between two and three hours: an evening is often a desirable period.
2. Throughout that time and in any situation that may develop you are to act and speak as you feel your partner acts and speaks. This is best done by taking separate turns, that is, Jill plays at being Jack for one evening, and then Jack plays at being Jill on the following evening. The person who is being mirrored is not to comment at the time on what his partner does or says in his name.

3. At the end of each session, the mirrored partner comments on the behavior of "himself" as portrayed by his partner.

What surprised you about your partner's acting?

What was expected?

Was any of the behavior exaggerated in your opinion?

What can you learn about yourself from the way in which your partner behaved? (a) How do you behave around the house? (b) How do you talk to your partner? (c) How do you spend an evening? (d) Who makes decisions, and about what? (e) How affectionate are you?

EXERCISE 6: *Getting Your Own Way*
Approximate time = one hour

For some couples, marriage is a battlefield where one person tries to outflank the other, split the opposing forces, win a Pyrrhic victory, outmaneuver, outrun and conquer the enemy. From time to time in every marriage, one person will wish to influence the other to agree to something he wants. How do we do this, and what effect does it have on our partner?

1. Jack decides on something that he wishes to influence Jill about, without telling Jill what it is.
2. He proceeds to try to get his own way behaving as he would normally. This continues until either he succeeds or he fails.
3. Jill comments on her feelings toward Jack, emanating from the techniques he used. Jill should be looking out for whether Jack tried to argue, persuade, threaten, cajole, bribe, wheedle, beg, etc.
4. Jack then comments on Jill's way of responding to his attempts to influence her. Did she get angry, listen attentively, laugh at him, try to make him feel guilty, etc.?
5. The exercise is repeated. This time it is Jill's turn to try to get her own way with Jack.

6. Summary. How did you both feel in the two roles? Which did you feel most comfortable with? Did you enjoy refusing to agree, or did you want to give in to please your partner, even at your own expense?

Satir and Shostrom[5] distinguish between four basic types of manipulative behavior:

Placating: pacifying, smoothing over differences, being nice, protective, covering up. "Oh, it's not so bad really," "We agree basically."
Avoiding: being quiet, pretending not to understand, changing the subject, playing weak and helpless. "I can't help it," "I didn't hear you."
Blaming: judging, bullying, comparing, complaining, "It's always your fault," "You never . . . ," "Why don't you . . ."
Preaching: lecturing, using outside authority, "You should . . . ," "You must . . . ," proving that you are right by explaining, calculating, masterminding, "Dr. Spock says . . . ," "What you're actually doing is . . ."

Which of these approaches do you think is applicable to you and your partner? Discuss this, and relate your discussion to the exercise you have just completed.

EXERCISE 7: *Appreciation*
Approximate time = thirty minutes

"He takes me for granted." How many times must that sentiment have been expressed? The horrible truth is that he probably does. We have written earlier on the predilection in our society to criticize people while forgetting to praise them.

5. Quoted in Stevens, *Awareness, op. cit.*

This simple exercise is designed to rectify this.

1. You say to your partner, "What I appreciate about you is . . ." See what words come out. Carry on until you can think of no more to say.
2. Ask your partner his feelings about what you have just said. What surprised him, what pleased him, did he feel anything was unjustified and if so, why?
3. Ask him to add anything which he thinks you might have said. Give your reactions to his additional reasons for wanting appreciation.
4. Repeat the exercise with your positions reversed

EXERCISE 8: *Resentment*
Approximate time = thirty minutes

Resentments sometimes build up in a marriage to such an extent that a creative relationship is impossible. Some people are afraid or ashamed to voice these resentments. This exercise will help you to communicate any resentments you have about your partner so that you will both be able to work on them.

1. You say to your partner, "What I resent about you is . . ." See what words come out. Censor the censor in your head. Continue until you feel you have exhausted all possible resentments.
2. Ask your partner her feelings about what you have said. What surprised her? What made her laugh? Did anything make her angry or sad? Did she feel anything was unjustified, and why?
3. What can the two of you do to help deal with these resentments, if they are found to be realistic? Be very careful here not to negate each other's perceptions.
4. Repeat the exercise with your roles reversed.

EXERCISE 9: *Expectations*

Approximate time = forty-five minutes

Throughout this book we have implied that many, if not the majority, of marital problems occur as a result of differences in expectations. This exercise is aimed at allowing some of these to rise to the surface of the relationship.

1. One person says to the other: "I expect you to . . ." Complete the sentence with whatever comes into your mind. It is important to be very specific about your expectations. Do not vaguely say, "I expect you to love me." You must say exactly in what ways you expect him to love you.
2. Your partner must repeat back the expectation, but without commenting on it.
3. Continue with your expectations until no more come to mind. A useful stimulus is to say the words "I expect you to . . .," even if you have no idea what words might follow.
4. Your partner discusses with you his reactions to your expectations—what surprised him, annoyed him, amused him, horrified him, etc.
5. Repeat the exercise with roles reversed.

EXERCISE 10: *"Excuse Me, but Haven't We Met Before?"*

Approximate time = thirty minutes

Many couples say that the one thing they miss, even in a very happy marriage, is the romance, the uncertainty, the thrust and parry of a new encounter with someone to whom they are attracted. We have heard many wives say, "Oh, if only he would seduce me like he used to"—immature and dangerously romantic, one might think, but they have a point. What they are really saying is that they feel they are taken for granted. Any freshness they feel is dissipated all too quickly by their husband's behavior which signifies that there is nothing new here that he does not know only too well. Familiarity breeds familiarity, and that can breed mediocrity if not contempt.

One way that couples reaffirm their feelings toward one another is to talk about their first and subsequent meetings of their courtship. This exercise is a role-playing one, where both partners attempt to act as if they do not know one another. The objective is try to step back from the familiarity of marriage to see your partner anew, to be aware of your feelings toward him, to notice what attracts you in his personality and in his physical appearance.

1. Decide on the situation. Is it to be a first meeting, or a first date following from a first meeting? Is it to be a replication of what really happened or a quite different situation? We would recommend the latter. This will make for freer role playing than if you are both trying avidly to remember "what happened next."
2. Play through the experience until it reaches a natural conclusion or until one of you decides to stop the role playing.
3. In addition to the objectives already mentioned, discuss who took the first move, how you reacted to one another—honestly, playfully, seductively, coolly, deceptively, etc. How much did you reveal about yourselves and your feelings, and how much did you keep hidden?
4. What did you learn or relearn from this experience about one another?

EXERCISE 11: *"Follow the Leader"*
Approximate time = evening/weekend/day

Many people find it difficult to give or receive instructions from their partner. This is usually because they are worried about being dominated or dominating. However, in the course of any relationship, to get the family work done it is helpful if spouses divide areas of work responsibility, and for each to be willing to cooperate by taking instructions from their partner in their partner's area of responsibility.[6] This is not meant to be taken rigidly, so that the man always empties the waste baskets and the woman always does the ironing. The actual tasks may be assigned first to one and then to the other on a future occasion if that is desired. But at any one time it will be most effective if one person takes the responsibility for a task.

This exercise provides an opportunity for each person to analyze his own reactions to leading and to being led.

1. Decide on a period of time for which one person will assume complete responsibility over how it is spent. At least a day or a weekend is preferable.
2. A coin is tossed to see who will be the decision maker.
3. The decision maker will then plan the time just as he wishes, assigning jobs, choosing where to go out and what to do. The follower can make no suggestions.

   Couples who try this sometimes find it very difficult especially if the first weekend is a reversal of the usual roles. Treating the whole affair humorously is perhaps the best way of handling it.
4. When the weekend is over, discuss what you have learned about: (a) your feelings when giving or receiving instructions; (b) your partner's competence in planning a weekend which is mutually enjoyable; (c) which jobs around the home cause greatest friction if the responsibility for carrying them out is reversed; (d) what irritates you about the way your partner gives instructions.
5. Repeat the session with the roles reversed.

6. This exercise is adapted from a similar one in Lederer and Jackson's *The Mirages of Marriage, op. cit.*

EXERCISE 12: *Let Us Agree to Disagree*
Approximate time = one hour

Any disagreement between two people provides an opportunity for learning something new about the topic of disagreement and about oneself.

If you have already completed a number of these exercises you will probably have found or underlined a number of things you disagree on, as well as discovering new areas of agreement. La Rochefoucauld claimed that "we seldom attribute common sense except to those who agree with us."

This exercise is designed to enable each person to express his common sense and to listen to the common sense of his partner.

1. Make a list, independently, of anything on which you feel that you and your partner disagree—values, beliefs, politics, religion, child rearing, domestic responsibility, etc.
2. Each person reads out his list, a discussion following each item.
3. If there is disagreement about whether an area of disagreement exists, discuss how this misperception could have occurred.
4. Be very specific about your disagreements.
5. Discuss your feelings about areas of disagreement.
6. How would your marriage be different if you did not disagree?

This last point is very important. Couples have discovered that sometimes the resolution of an area of disagreement would only slightly affect their marriage. It is too easy to assume that people have to agree on everything from whether God exists to how to cut one's toenails before they can have a satisfactory marriage. The important question is whether the disagreement affects the way you live together or is just a personal affront to one's "common sense." If it is the latter, you might ask yourself just what you are afraid of that makes you feel threatened by an opposing belief or point of view. There are, undoubtedly, certain areas of disagreement that cause considerable strain on a marriage, for example, birth control. It is vital to obtain this information before marriage. You then have to decide whether or not you can tolerate that difference.

EXERCISE 13: *Mood Manufacture*
Approximate time = one hour

Everyone's mood changes from time to time. In most marriages one person's moods will often tend to dictate, to some extent, their partner's moods. A person with more extreme moods is likely to dictate the climatic mood of the home more than a person who is less changeable.

This exercise will provide you with data on what moods your partner thinks you are subject to and how they affect him.

1. Each person, independently, writes down a list of the other partner's moods—anger, sulkiness, ebullience, etc.
2. Read out your lists to one another. Try to give a recent example to support each assertion.
3. See how far it is possible to create a mood in yourself of (a) happiness, (b) anger, (c) lovingness. What did you do to create this? How much control do you have over your moods?
4. Do you have any moods you would rather not experience? What gives rise to these? How far can you create another mood to override this? Can your partner help to create this second mood?

EXERCISE 14: *Sharing Sex Fantasies*
Approximate time = one hour

The majority of people fantasize about sex—when they are not getting it, when they are getting it, and when they are right in the middle of it. A counselor's casebook teems with guilt feelings caused by fantasies about sexual activities. However, it is quite normal for men and women to have fantasies, and often quite extraordinary ones at that. Men worry about having occasional homosexual fantasies, yet there is nothing unusual about this. Only if they have no other fantasies might there be some significance. We have known people who, whatever criteria were used, would be classed as being quite normal. Yet they have admitted fantasies of lesbianism, homosexuality, group sex, extramarital affairs with known people, bestiality, sadistic-masochistic episodes, countless fetishes ranging from rubberwear through bondage to transvestitism, sex with children, incest with parents and children, and many others. In all of these examples, the fantasies, although recurring periodically, were not constant, and the only harm they generated was when they caused conscious worry.

Husbands and wives typically feel very guilty about having sexual fantasies, especially during their love making, yet sharing fantasies could make their sex life more enjoyable and their relationship more open. Allowing your thoughts to move as freely as your body can heighten the total experience. However, disclosing your fantasies without warning could be disturbing to your partner. This is why it is essential to create the appropriate climate for this.

1. Each partner shares with the other (a) one sexual fantasy he has experienced during their love making; (b) one sexual fantasy he has experienced at some time other than when they are making love.
2. Examine one another's reactions to these fantasies. Each person answers the question: "Does this fantasy mean that I desire you less?"
3. Share any other sexual fantasies you can recall and feel comfortable in discussing.
4. Would you like to translate any of these fantasies into actuality?

For the majority of people, most fantasies serve their purpose kept on that level. At the height of sexual ardor it might be tempting to translate the images into practice, but posttumescence, most people are happy to keep them as fantasies.

What would be the implications of putting them into practice for both of you?

Some couples discover that fantasies involving their partners are capable of being put into practice and they experiment with these, for example, oral intercourse, some form of dressing up, making love in unusual positions or places, and even in partner swapping and troilism. As long as each person knows the effects of his actions on his partner and the partner is also eager to explore new possibilities, then they are unlikely to come to grief. But it is very tempting for a dominant person to persuade his partner to do something of which the latter is uncertain or even disapproving.

Explore your fantasies together. Enjoy them. Use your partner sexually, and allow your partner to use you. Talk about your feelings when you are used and when you do the using.

Navran[7] found in studying communication between happily and unhappily married couples that, in descending order of importance, the happily marrieds differed from their unhappy counterparts in that they:

1. *Much more frequently talked over pleasant things that happened during the day.*

2. *Felt more frequently understood by their spouse.*

3. *Discussed things in which they were both interested.*

4. *Were less likely to break off communication or inhibit it by sulking.*

5. *More often talked with each other about personal problems.*

7. Leslie Navran, "Communication and Adjustment in Marriage," *Family Process,* 6 (1967), 173–184.

6. *Made more frequent use of words which had a private meaning for them.*

7. *Generally talked most things over.*

8. *Were more sensitive to each other's feelings and took these into account when speaking.*

9. *Were freer to discuss intimate issues without restraint or embarrassment.*

10. *Were more able to tell what kind of day their spouses had without asking.*

11. *Communicated nonverbally to a greater degree, via the exchange of glances.*

NONVERBAL COMMUNICATION

EXERCISE 15: *Nonverbal Introduction*
Approximate time = thirty minutes

Exercise 10 allowed two people to encounter each other afresh. The medium was words. This time, the encounter will be nonverbal.

1. Using a blindfold, or simply keeping your eyes closed, sit opposite your partner, but close enough to touch him without difficulty. Using your hands only, explore his head and hands. Do not speak. Your partner is to offer no resistance. Continue for as long as you think is necessary to enable a complete encounter with your partner.

2. Discuss the thoughts and feelings that you experienced when encountering your partner.
   Did you enjoy touching him?
   If you did, what parts did you enjoy touching the most?
   What could you discover about your partner from this nonverbal encounter?

Was he enjoying it?

Describe your partner from how he felt to you.

3. Repeat, allowing your partner to encounter you.

EXERCISE 16: *"I Can Read You Like a Book"*
Approximate time = one week

In living with someone from day to day we learn our partner's ways of communicating his thoughts, feelings and moods. Sometimes he discusses them. At other times he indicates them by a whole series of subtle and not-so-subtle nonverbal actions.

"Whenever John comes home from work and doesn't bother to change his clothes, I know he's in a bad mood."

"When I get home and see Sarah with her long hair pulled back with an elastic band, I know that she's feeling depressed."

"If Anne talks and laughs loudly with the children I know that she is happy. If she doesn't interact much with them, then she is unhappy."

We have found that most people can indicate a number of nonverbal signals like those just mentioned, but only in relation to their partner. People are not usually so observant about their own behavior.

This exercise is designed to help you be more receptive to the ways in which your partner communicates nonverbally to you and other people, and how you communicate to others.

1. After agreeing to do the exercise, each person notes down any nonverbal signals that they see their partner communicating both to them and to other people. This is done over a period of seven days.

2. At the end of one week, each person sits down and shares his list with his partner.

How many of these signals were each of you aware of communicating at the time?

How many of the nonverbal communications were (a) happy or positive, and (b) unhappy or negative?

Caution: There is often a tendency to notice only the negative signals. Be on the lookout for the positive ones too. These are more easily missed. Do not enter into competition to discover who can obtain the biggest list of "nasty" messages.

EXERCISE 17: *Voice Listening*
Approximate time = fifteen minutes

One of the most important nonverbal message carriers is the human voice—not the words which are spoken, but the manner of delivery, tone, pitch, volume and accent. What does the sound of your partner's voice communicate to you?

1. Each person chooses a poem or piece of prose to read out loud to the other.
2. When your partner begins to read, try to forget the content, close your eyes and just listen to the voice.

What sort of person owns that voice?

What range of emotions is expressed?
3. Share your perceptions with your partner.
4. Your partner now listens to your recital.

EXERCISE 18: *Gobbledegook*
Approximate time = fifteen minutes

1. You are now to talk to your partner in a nonsense language. Using only gibberish you are to try to communicate the following emotions:

Joy
Sadness
Silliness
Anger
Irritability
Embarrassment
Pleasure
Affection
Passion
Any other emotions you would like to convey

Do not communicate them in this order, because your partner will next be trying to communicate the same emotions to you.

2. After each expression, ask your partner which emotion you were conveying. Ask him why he thought it was one emotion rather than any other. What were the cues to which he was responding? Was he just concentrating on the sound of your voice, or were other factors involved like eye contact, eyebrow movement, mouth movements, head actions, etc.?

3. Repeat for your partner.

EXERCISE 19: *Pushing*
Approximate time = ten minutes

All married couples have to work out where they stand in terms of dominance and submission. Is one person always to be dominant? Will one person be dominant in one area of married life and be submissive in other areas? Is one person to be dominant in one area sometimes and yet submissive at others? In what manner are these issues to be solved?

This exercise should open these questions to discussion.

1. Jack faces Jill. Both are standing. He puts his hands on her shoulders and attempts to force her to the ground.
2. Jill tries to force Jack to the ground in the same way.

3. What happens? Are your responses typical of your reactions when you make demands on one another?

I must do these things in order to communicate:
Become aware of you (discover you),
Make you aware of me (uncover myself),
Be ready to change during our conversation,
and be willing to reveal my changes to you.
For communication to have meaning it must have a life. It must transcend "you and me" and become "us." If I truly communicate, I see in you a life that is not me and partake of it. And you see and partake of me. In a small way we then grow out of our old selves and become something new. To have this kind of sharing I cannot enter a conversation clutching myself. I must enter it with loose boundaries. I must give myself to the relationship, *and be willing to be what grows out of it.*

Hugh Prather

---

6 · Trust

Intimacy is a road and not a goal.

Charlotte and Howard Clinebell

Usually at the heart of games playing and manipulation ploys in marriage lies the problem of trust. Do I trust her? What will he do to me if he possesses this knowledge about me? Will he leave me if he knows how much I need him? Will she hurt me if she realizes how much power she has over me?

It is rare for a couple to be completely honest with each other all the time. Indeed, it is questionable if this is always desirable. In the section on giving feedback[1] we suggested that honesty for honesty's sake may satisfy the discloser but may be destructive for the receiver. Negative feedback is only useful if the recipient really wants it and if he is in a position to change his behavior as a result of it. Telling your wife that her ears stick out too far is not helpful to anyone, to say the least.

However, marriages in which people are open about their love and anger, in which conflicts are confronted and affection expressed, are most likely to satisfy a wide range of needs and to be flexible in the face of change. It is because people change that trust is sometimes obliterated. We are frightened that if our partner changes we will be left behind. Undoubtedly, people do change. Between young adulthood and middle age

1. Pp. 33–45.

married couples change considerably. After twenty years couples have been shown to change 52 percent of their values, 55 percent of their vocational interests, 69 percent of their self-rated personality characteristics and 92 percent of their answers to attitude questions.[2] A marriage cannot be static because people are not static. Unless these individual changes are discussed it will be difficult for the marriage to incorporate them. Faced with these difficulties, some people are afraid of honesty because of the fear of being unable to cope with its consequences. They play games in which they pretend that nothing has changed in the marriage or that the change is of no consequence. There is little to be gained from self or other deceit.

When I am honestly myself, and you respond warmly and with caring, then love exists. If I calculate and put on phoney behaviour in order to please you, you may love my behaviour but you cannot love me, because I have hidden my real existence behind this artificial behaviour. Even when you love in response to my phoney behaviour, I cannot really receive your love. It is poisoned by my knowledge that the love is for the image I have created, not for me. I also have to be continually on guard to be sure that I maintain my image so that your love does not disappear. Since I have shut myself off from your love in this way, I will feel more lonely and unloved, and try even more desperately to manipulate myself and you in order to get this love.[3]

There has been an accumulation of research findings over the past ten years[4] which suggests that people who disclose

2. E. Lowell Kelly, "Consistency of the Adult Personality," *American Psychologist*, 10 (1955), 654–681.
3. Stevens, *Awareness, op. cit.*, p. 88.
4. For a review of this work consult Sidney Jourard's *Self-Disclosure*, Wiley, New York, 1971.

themselves to others are considerably healthier psychologically than those who do not reveal themselves. The "strong silent types" in our culture are more likely to end up strong, silent, neurotic types. It is also very clear that by being *yourself* to others, they are more likely to be *themselves* with you: self-disclosure begets self-disclosure. By trusting another person with information about yourself, you are taking the first step to building up your self-esteem. If he accepts you, the *real* you, the value of your existence has been confirmed by at least one other person. The tragedy is that so many of us think of ourselves as being of little value and feel that if others really knew us they would agree. Most people who take the risk of self-disclosure find that, on the contrary, people feel warmer toward them. Disclosing intimacies creates a bond.

The important prerequisite for self-disclosure is trust.

DON'T BE WARY OF YOUR PARTNER—BE AWARE

This chapter provides a series of exercises that will help you to discover more about how trusting and trustworthy you are; how you react in situations where trust is called for; how to build a trusting climate in your marriage.

EXERCISE 1: *Blind Man's Walk*
Approximate time = thirty minutes

How far do you really trust your partner—in the sense of being able to rely upon him completely never to let you down? Your answer to this will be partly dictated by circumstances, but will mainly reflect your overall trust level. Some people are naturally more trusting than others. Sometimes they are taken advantage of, but in practice most people discover that this rarely happens. For every negative experience there will be scores of positive ones which could have been lost for fear of experiencing the one negative effect.

This exercise will help you to answer the questions: "How easily am I able to trust my entire person with my partner?" "Can I learn anything from this experience which says something about the way in which I relate generally to people?"

It is a nonverbal exercise and consequently aimed at bypassing many of the verbal concepts which we carry around about ourselves as trusting or untrusting people.

1. One of you blindfolds the other. You then take your partner on a walk for five to ten minutes during which time no verbal communication may pass between you. Try to ensure that you have stairs to contend with and differences of texture to walk upon. Take your partner outside the house.
2. After the walk, do not discuss your feelings or thoughts, but simply reverse positions.
3. After both of you have completed the walk, ask each other the following questions: "How easy did you find it to relax with me when guiding and being guided?" "What feelings did you have when guiding me and being guided by me?" "What techniques did you use to guide me?"

Couples often discover that this exercise says much about their ability to take complete responsibility for another person and to hand themselves over to someone else.

> "I realized that I was tense when Jeff guided me. I couldn't let myself go. It's not that I don't trust him. I think it's because in my family, and also with Jeff, I am always the one who was expected to be responsible. I just can't get used to the idea of letting others look after me."
>
> "Sue completely relaxed when I guided her. This I found frightening. The power that I had. I could have let her fall downstairs, possibly kill herself. I realized that I don't like

responsibility, and this is something I want to change in myself. I want to be more like Sue, who was relaxed when in charge of me, but also was able to relax when I was looking after her."

"I felt that Bob was constantly going to let go of me. And once he did, and he laughed. I think this does say something about us. I never feel that I could rely on Bob if I got into any sort of trouble. More likely than not he would say it was my fault anyway."

4. Does this exercise help you to say anything about your typical response to people?

EXERCISE 2: *"Take Me, I'm Yours!"*
Approximate time = thirty minutes

The rationale for this exercise is the same as for the previous one. Again, the approach is nonverbal.

1. One of you lies on the floor, while the other kneels by your side, and relaxes you using the tension-relaxation part of the relaxation exercise described earlier. You then tell your partner to close his eyes: "I am now going to ask you to give complete control of your arm to me. I want you to trust me. I will not hurt you."

Then place one hand beneath your partner's upper arm, and your other hand under his wrist. Do not hold, simply support. Raise the arm gently but firmly off the ground. Move it around. Take it across his face. Change direction. Do what you like but remember your promise not to hurt him. Gradually return his arm to the floor.

2. Ask him to discuss his feelings. The sensation itself is sometimes described as rather weird. Many people report that they had little idea of where their arm was being moved to.

Discuss your feelings about how it felt to be given his arm. Did he give it completely? Was it relaxed? Was he anticipating your moves? What does this say about his ability to trust you?

3. Reverse positions.
4. Now do the same exercise, this time lifting the head with both hands, from a kneeling position behind his head. Some people who are able to let go of their arm quite easily find the head a different proposition. It is more valuable than an arm. It weighs more. If it is dropped, it will hurt more.

Discuss your feelings as "lifter" and "lifted."

5. Reverse positions and do the exercise again.

EXERCISE 3: *"I Have a Secret"*
Approximate time = thirty minutes

Most couples have secrets which they have not disclosed to each other in case their partner loses respect for them or is shocked or the marriage is put at risk. Factors like adultery and homosexuality are usually the ones that are riskiest for most marriages, although where these are openly discussed the marriage is occasionally strengthened. At least, if a marriage *can* weather the devastating impact of such a disclosure—and it would be foolish to underestimate the degree of maturity and faith which that will demand—the relationship, almost by definition, becomes a more stable one. The more individual differences are incorporated into a partnership, the smaller the chances will be of toppling the partnership at the onset of further revelations. We are not going to suggest that you admit to your extramarital sexual activities. Without the guidance of a skilled counselor this could trigger off a situation which neither of you could control. This is not to say that you should not risk this, but it is a very important warning.

1. One person begins by saying: "I have a secret. I have never told you before that . . ."

2. His partner then confides a secret of her own.
3. This continues until each cannot think of any more secrets that they can or wish to confide.
4. Discuss reactions to these. Have your feelings about one another changed?
5. Does this exercise have any implications for how you interact with people generally?

EXERCISE 4: *"What I Really Think about Our Marriage"*
Approximate time = one hour

Earlier in this book we made the point that, generally, people in our culture are self-critical. With "friends" like we are to ourselves we do not need enemies! As we look at ourselves critically, so we tend to concentrate on the negative aspects of our marriage. The longer people have been married, the fewer favorable qualities they tend to see in each other.[5] In other words, the image has tarnished. Among the virtues which fade are affection, consideration, cooperation, gratitude and friendliness. Instead, the spouse tends to be increasingly perceived as selfish, bitter, touchy, hard-hearted, cold and unfeeling. This is hardly a climate in which to nourish trust, which is always a delicate bloom.

This exercise is designed to help you obtain a realistic *and* comprehensive picture of your marriage.

Each person answers the following questions:

1. The best things about our marriage are . . .
2. What do I feel is important in a marriage? How many of these qualities does our marriage possess?
3. How can I improve our marriage?
4. What must you do to help me improve our marriage?

Make an action plan designed to make changes in your

5. Eleanor B. Luckey, "Number of Years Married as Related to Personality, Perception and Marital Satisfaction," *Journal of Marriage and the Family,* 28 (1966), 44–48.

behavior over the next few weeks. Do not plan to do things which will be extremely difficult to achieve. Be specific.

EXERCISE 5: *Self-disclosure*
Approximate time = one hour

This is the chance to really lay yourself on the line and see if the train stops in time.
Each person answers the following questions:

1. Describe fully the people with whom you have been in love, excluding your present partner.
2. Describe the kind of people with whom you would most like to have sexual experiences.
3. Why do some people dislike you?
4. What are your best points?
5. How satisfied are you with the different parts of your body?
6. What aspects of your personality do you worry about, dislike, or regard as a handicap to yourself?
7. How sexually adequate do you think you are?
8. What actions have you most regretted in your life, and why?
9. Whom do you resent most in your life, and why?
10. What do you really think about your in-laws?
11. What do you like and dislike about your children?

After each question there may be discussion before proceeding. The final question is:

12. Do you feel that you know more about each other as a result of this exercise?

To be of central significance to a partner means to be close; to share the peak moments of a lifetime as well as the trivial ups and downs of daily existence; to be included and brought into the private world of feelings, wants and fears of the other; to care and fuss about the other's growth, his triumphs and frustrations, his lot in life; to identify and empathize with his ways of being and growing; to be fussed over and cared about by him; to have a partner for sharing one's private concerns about oneself, about life, growing, succeeding, failing; to give and take pleasure and to facilitate on each other a sense of well-being; to enjoy the safety of a private harbor in a sea of troubles.

George Bach and Peter Wyden[6]

6. *The Intimate Enemy, op. cit.*

7 · Your Relationship: A Time and Emotion Study

American research on marriage suggests that one in three people, if given the choice, would not marry the same person again. One in nine British marriages and one in four American marriages end in divorce. Many marriages consist of "standing" relationships only. They give both partners marital *standing* in the community; "My wife does not under*stand* me" and "I can't *stand* my husband." The brave or desperate get out; the more apathetic or insecure live in the shadows of their former dreams. Some of this unhappiness is inevitable because of an immature or unfortunate choice of partner or because of external pressures on the relationship which could not have been predicted. However, we would maintain that many marriages turn sour because people on the whole find it easier to embark on a new relationship than they do to develop or change their existing one. The task of coping with marital problems, some of which will be long-standing, can appear enormous compared to the relatively simple task of starting afresh with someone new. As members of the "throw-away" society, we have been told by our technicians that it is easier to replace a malfunctioning part in its entirety than to invest time in tinkering with a small part of its mechanism. Similarly, there is an increasing tendency to throw away our problems instead of trying to resolve them.

The exercises presented in this chapter are a challenge to

couples to explore to the full the possibility of satisfying some of their own needs *through* their relationship, rather than in spite of it.

In our experience, some couples are astonished at how much their needs do overlap, while others are disturbed by the extent to which they are excluded from their partner's life. The fact that you are doing these exercises together suggests that you do want to share your lives and therefore you are most likely to discover that you fit into the first category. But if you do find that you have plans which exclude each other, this is best recognized and worked upon.

Are sleeping dogs ever best left lying? Not if the lying involves telling lies. These exercises cannot render a satisfactory relationship unsatisfactory. What they might do, however, is to reveal a situation in which one partner is not satisfied by the relationship, but is not admitting this to himself or his partner. At best, the relationship will be improved by facing up to the reality of each partner's feelings. At worst, the couple may have to admit that their needs are incompatible. This in itself does not register the end of the marriage. Marriages do exist where both partners have incompatible needs and yet each would say that their marriage was an overall success. It must be left to each couple to decide for themselves in how many areas of their marriage they are prepared to accept genuine conflict.

One of the major objectives of this book is to demonstrate the constructive use of conflict (see page 80), and the following exercises are perhaps the most powerful ones in the book. The exercises to date are intended to help you to discover who you are, who your partner is, how much you trust one another and how well you communicate. This exercise is designed to answer the question, "Okay, now we know who we are in relation to each other, but where do we go from here?"

For all of us, the time and energy we have to invest is limited. People will often take considerable trouble before investing their money in stocks, a house or a new car. They want to know what return they will get on their capital and they will assiduously compare products before coming to a decision. However, these same people will often invest their time and energy haphazardly without regard to the return they are getting. One's life provides one with a progressively diminishing amount of time to invest, but as with all good investments, there is no reason for the returns to dwindle.

The objectives of this time and emotion study are:

1. To discover what your needs are in life.
2. To find out what really satisfies you and dissatisfies you.
3. To determine how you invest your time and emotional energy.
4. To see if this investment is the most effective way of satisfying your needs.
5. To plan ways of using limited time and energy so that as many as possible of your own and each other's needs are satisfied.

TIME AND EMOTION STUDY

Parts 1–8 are completed by both partners. They write down their responses to each question, independently of each other.

1. Peak Experiences

Write down any event or series of events in the time you have spent together which you would call "peak experiences." These will be the high spots of your relationship. They could have occurred before or after marriage, and can cover any area of your life together. Carry out the following procedure for each peak experience:

a. Say what it was.
b. Describe what happened.

c. Discuss your feelings about it (but not yet with your partner).

d. Do you think your partner was aware of your feelings at
the time?

e. Do you think your partner felt the same way?

2. Trough Experiences

Repeat exercise 1, except that you should now try to recall
anything that has happened in your life together which you
would call a "trough experience." These will indicate the low
points of your relationship.

3. Future Experiences

What experiences have you not shared with your partner
that you would like to? These might be of major or minor
importance—like having a child or eating at a new restaurant.

4. Fantasy Day

In our culture, fantasy has a decidedly negative connota-
tion. It is associated with "daydreaming," which is seen as
pointless and not conducive to "getting things done." On the
contrary, we would claim that fantasy experiences, apart from
often being highly enjoyable, can be very creative and can
generate insights into our deeply felt needs and anxieties.
Fantasizing can give us hope, for without hope there is no
ambition. It is only destructive when used as a substitute for
action, but it can be a potent stimulus to action.

One of the sad facts of human development in our culture
is that as we grow older we forget how to play. Fantasy is a
form of play, and as such we feel it is justifiable in its own
right. Moreover, sharing one's fantasies is one way of sharing
oneself with others. We can feel joy and sadness by participat-
ing in someone else's fantasy, while conveying our own feelings to them through our own fantasies. In this way it is

possible to develop a new perspective through which to view ourselves and others. Fantasy can release parts of ourselves that have been imprisoned by the "dailiness" of living. It can be a powerful generator of human potential.

You have twenty-four hours to spend with your partner in any way you like. Your money is unlimited, and you may begin your twenty-four hours in any part of the world. However, traveling time must be taken into account during your fantasy day. For instance, if you begin in Tahiti, it will take most of your remaining time to travel to Finland.

You should write down chronologically exactly what you would like to do in your partner's company throughout the twenty-four hours. The time period may begin at any moment you choose—for example, from midnight to midnight or from eight o'clock one morning until eight o'clock the following morning.

5. Fantasy Life

As well as daydreaming, we often spend time "lifedreaming." Some people can conjure up a variety of different lives they would enjoy living. This exercise is an attempt to encourage you to focus on what your ideal life with your partner would be like. It can encompass any period of time you wish —a span of one or fifty years. For your fantasy life experience, you need to answer the following questions:

a. What sort of person would you be?
b. What sort of person would your partner be?
c. Describe the lives you would both be living.

6. Marital Obituary

You are to imagine that your marriage has ended, through the death of one partner or because you have divorced. Your marriage is to be described in the manner of an obituary:

a. Describe your marriage from beginning to end. In other words, project yourself into the future moment at which your marriage ends. Now describe what has actually happened in reality and continue with a description of the rest of your marriage, between now and its imagined end.

b. Ask yourself the following question: Do these descriptions sum up what I want from my marriage?

c. If the last answer was "yes," then no further comment is necessary. If the answer was "no," then describe how you would *like* the obituary to read.

7. *Marriage Lines*

Draw a line to represent your marriage. Put a mark to indicate where you are on the line. Draw the line in any way you like and then explain it.

8. *Life Investment Record*

Take the last week of your life, if that has been reasonably representative of your life together. If not, take a recent week that was fairly typical. The object of the exercise is to work out how you spend your time. You can do this by filling in the compartments in the Life Investment Record reproduced below.

Life investment record

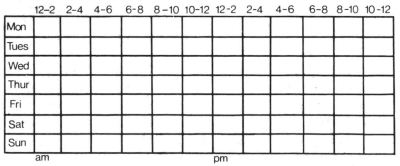

	12–2	2–4	4–6	6–8	8–10	10–12	12–2	2–4	4–6	6–8	8–10	10–12
Mon												
Tues												
Wed												
Thur												
Fri												
Sat												
Sun												

am   pm

You can begin your week on any day.

Work out the percentage of time you spend on each activity. You can either construct your own list to fit the various activities in your life, or use the list provided as a general guideline:

% of time spent sleeping (this is not necessarily the same as being in bed!).

% of time spent at home, other than sleeping.

% of time spent in employment.

% of time doing work around the house.

% of time spent with partner alone at home.

% of time spent with partner outside the home.

% of time with friends.

% of time with children.

% of time spent watching television.

% of time spent pursuing interest or hobby.

and so on . . .

Looking at the results, are you satisfied with the way you allocate your time?

Is your relationship likely to be helped by the fact that you probably have a better idea of where your time goes?

Is there any way you could reallocate your time to satisfy more of your needs, and specifically help your marriage?

9. Sharing

After the first eight parts of this exercise have been completed, each person shares his findings with his partner. This is best done in the following manner:

a. John shares his peak and trough experiences with Jill, who is not allowed to comment at this stage. She is allowed to ask for clarification of points she does not understand.

b. Jill comments on John's experiences.

c. Jill then shares her peak and trough experiences with John, who is only allowed to ask for clarification.
d. John comments on Jill's experiences.
e. They discuss what they have learned about each other's perception of their marriage, and what the most important aspects of the marriage are for each of them.

This technique of listening without comment, then commenting, followed by a discussion of "What does this mean for us?" is used throughout this sharing exercise.

It is important to abide by this technique as all too often a marital discussion develops into an argument with neither partner listening, and the air becomes filled with abuse, abandon and abomination. The skills involved in effective listening are discussed earlier.

The trouble with a disagreeable wife is that she makes you angry. The trouble with an agreeable wife is that she makes you think instead.

Eric Berne

John and Jill next share their ideas about future experiences in the same way. They also share their fantasy days. We have found this to be a particularly revealing exercise. For example, some people are horrified to discover that their partner did not include their children in their twenty-four hours. The maxim here, as throughout, is:

EXPLORATION NOT CONDEMNATION

With a certain amount of sensitivity it is possible to learn a great deal about a partner's needs from his descriptions.

The fantasy life exercise is often revealing. It allows people to explore the significance of their more long-term daydreams. In our experience, fantasies have ranged from the subject imagining himself to be an international negotiator to being a market gardener, from being a high-court judge to being a high-wire performer, and from being a mother of three to being a member of a commune with a choice of three sleeping partners.

The marital obituary is designed to search out people's expectations for the future as well as to record their perceptions of the past. Sometimes a couple's accounts of the past appear not to refer to the same marriage. This usually reflects very different needs brought to the marriage by each partner. This, in conjunction with the marriage lines, is designed to force a couple to ask themselves and each other just what they want from their marriage in the future. It also makes the point that you *do* have control over what happens to your marriage. Everyone has freedom to maneuver, yet so many married people think that they have no alternative to the existing life style they have established for themselves.

The life investment record is designed to demonstrate just how much freedom to maneuver most people have (at least in terms of time). Presumably, you should be spending as much time as possible on the things you would label "top priority" in your life. Several of the exercises have forced you to decide what your priorities are. The life investment record should help you to match these priorities to the time you have at your disposal, so that you get as much as you can from your marriage.

Many people are genuinely shocked by seeing just how their time and energy is divided. One individual discovered that out of the week's total of 168 hours, he spent 30 hours watching television. This was about 20 percent of his total week, 30 percent of his waking hours and 80 percent of the waking time he spent at home. He claimed that he and his wife never talked, and one of his peak experiences was watching a TV show on Saturday nights. As a result of the exercise, he and his wife had a great deal of talking to do, and he rescheduled a large proportion of his home activities.

Many husbands are amazed to see how much time their wives spend working around the house. "A woman's work is never done" is well supported by research findings. These indicate that a full-time housewife with no children will probably work a 40–60-hour week; a housewife with one child between 60 and 70 hours a week; a housewife with two children between 70 and 80 hours a week. If these same women were employed outside the home, they would probably spend respectively 30, 40 and 50 hours a week on housework, in addition to the time spent in their nondomestic work. Being presented with these facts in black and white has been known to turn husbands pale and suburban housewives into ardent supporters of women's liberation.

For those interested in how their use of leisure time compares with that in Britain, the illustration on the next page gives the facts.

These figures do not account for age or social-class differences. Other studies have shown that the lower the socioeconomic status, the greater the proportion of leisure time spent watching television; the higher the social class, the greater the participation in physical recreation. Interestingly, attendance at spectator sports is the same across the complete span of social classes. As for age, young people spend more time in physical recreation (including dancing) and less watching television. After marriage, this pattern changes to a predominance of gardening and do-it-yourself activities for men, and crafts and hobbies (mainly knitting) for women.

10. Plans for Action

You have now collected a good deal of information about your marriage. You should have a better idea of what sort of

Use of leisure time

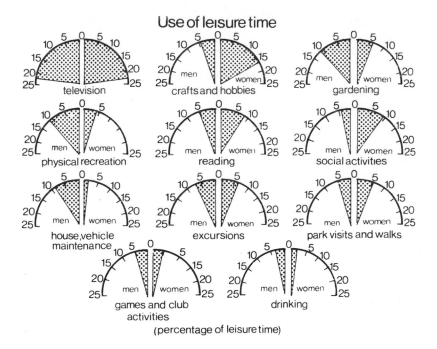

television

crafts and hobbies

gardening

physical recreation

reading

social activities

house, vehicle maintenance

excursions

park visits and walks

games and club activities

drinking

(percentage of leisure time)

creature it is, in terms of how much it works for you and how much you work for it. The question to be answered now is, what do you plan to do to develop your marriage?

If more time is called for, you can see how this can be gained by consulting your life investment record.

Many people find it useful, after completing the exercise, to list a number of things they wish to do, achieve or change, say, in the next six months, in order to improve the relationship. These objectives are discussed and then placed in a sealed envelope. An entry is made in a family diary to the effect that the envelope is to be opened six months hence. The couple can then check up on how many of their good intentions have been put into operation. Examples of these from

1. Alan F. Sillitoe, *Britain in Figures: A Handbook of Social Statistics,* Penguin Books Ltd., Harmondsworth, 1971.

our group work experience illustrate a range of problems including the following:

To spend twice as much time doing things together.

To consult some sex manuals in an attempt to introduce more variety into the couple's sex life.

To spend half as much time watching television, and to use it, instead, for talking or reading.

To consult a marriage guidance counselor where the couple felt incapable of solving their own problems.

To buy a camper for weekends together.

To take up part-time employment as an antidote to housewifely depression.

To take up a hobby that both partners could share.

One of the leading characters in Iris Murdoch's novel *A Severed Head* says to his wife, "We aren't getting anywhere. You know that as well as I do." To which she replies, "One doesn't have to get anywhere in a marriage. It's not a public conveyance." But marriage can be a vehicle for the personal growth of both partners, and each needs to take a turn at the wheel.

8·Would You Marry the Same Person Again?

The old music-hall joke goes, "Marriage is a very fine institution, but who wants to live in an institution?" People are quick to make light of subjects that they may in fact feel strongly about. Hence the preponderance of jokes about sex, death, women, Negroes and Jews. And hence the frequency with which cynical comments about marriage are made.

The likening of marriage to an institution is an interesting reflection of the way people perceive marriage. It suggests that people associate marriage with a loss of freedom. Men still talk as if it were a trap. Jonathan Swift said, "The reason why so few marriages are happy is because young ladies spend their time in making nets, not in making cages." The assumption persists that at the announcement of an engagement, the woman is to be congratulated and the man commiserated with.

Jonathan Swift's words are also appropriate to another attitude to marriage, held by many girls—that it is the same thing as a wedding day. For many, courtship is a time for planning how to keep the wedding guests happy on the wedding day, rather than on how to keep one's partner and oneself happy for the rest of one's life. The wedding day is seen to be the culmination of everything, rather than the beginning of something of huge potential. Marriage is not an immovable "fact of life," like a cell with four concrete walls against which the prisoner bangs his head but whose form he can never hope to change. To take on the role of marriage partner is to undertake an ongoing, ever-changing, give-and-take transaction which will depend for its stability and satisfaction not only on the two people involved but on many other factors, some of which will be inevitably and constantly changing. The role of spouse is not one of prisoner, at the mercy of more powerful forces. It is one of sculptor—unable to change the basic nature of his stone, but with the opportunity to choose its form.

However tempting it is to be cynical about marriage, the fact remains that a greater proportion of the population is marrying than ever before. Only 5 percent of teenage boys in 1970 and 4 percent of girls will remain unmarried. And of those who do divorce, two-thirds will marry again, a fact which reflects "the triumph of hope over experience," as Samuel Johnson put it. But in spite of the impression sometimes conveyed by the mass media, by far the majority of marriages last a lifetime.

In 1970 over 50,000 marriages in the United Kingdom ended in divorce. Approximately one in nine enters the divorce courts. In the United States one marriage in every four does not last. The individual's response to these figures—whether of shock, smugness, or indifference—will depend on his values. Those who feel that the institution of marriage is essential for the maintenance of the style of life typical of the West will be horrified. Others may feel that, in view of the increasing permissiveness of Western society, these figures could be much worse. Some will remain indifferent, taking the view that marital breakdown in itself is not disastrous. If a marriage satisfies two people for ten years and then ceases to fulfill their needs, is that marriage a failure? In terms of divorce statistics it certainly is. In terms of human happiness experienced, the issue is debatable.

For anyone examining marital breakdown (a less value-loaded concept than "failure"), the major problem lies in defining just what is meant by "breakdown." Divorce statistics are a significant but limited indicator. If a marriage does not end in divorce, can one be sure that the marriage has not "broken down"? Few people would be entirely satisfied with the assumption that it had not; the couple may not even be living under the same roof.

Visible breakdown must include separations, but these may be only temporary. They still provide evidence of the degree of marital dissatisfaction in the society, however. An English study, which traced a sample of couples married between 1930 and 1949, found that between 6 and 10 percent had experienced an episode of separation, and 5 to 7 percent had terminated in divorce. Some 2 to 4 percent had contemplated separation. Thus, between 8 and 14 percent of the couples admitted to marital problems which were serious enough at least to contemplate separation, if not actually experience separation or seek a divorce.

It is more difficult to find statistical evidence of masked breakdown. A couple may remain living together "because of the children" or because divorce would harm the husband's career or because it would mean a loss of status for the wife within the community. Inertia may also play an important part in keeping couples together. It is sometimes "easier" to put up with an unsatisfactory marriage than to suffer the public comments, insecurities and sheer hard work involved in obtaining a divorce. Many people who readily admit to their marriage being a disaster have never considered the possibility of divorce. This is more often the case when there has been no previous history of divorce in either family and when marital expectations are low. One young wife's comment probably reflects the way many people think: "I didn't expect a lot from marrying Pete. I mean you have to get married, don't you? And he seemed a clean, respectable type. I suppose I could have done worse. We're no worse off than Mom and Dad."

One effective technique for discovering the extent of marital dissatisfaction in a society is to ask the question "Would you marry the same person again?" Research carried out in the United States suggests that up to one in three spouses would not choose the same partner again. This suggests that the incidence of masked breakdown is extremely high. If marital breakdown statistics allow for this, then it is probably not too farfetched to suggest that at least 50 percent of marriages in the United Kingdom and the United States are unsatisfactory temporarily, or even permanently.

A further problem in looking at marital breakdown concerns the question of who is to decide just what constitutes a successful marriage. An investigator who believes that a successful marriage involves both partners discussing their problems with each other, understanding one another and sharing their marital roles would class as unsatisfactory a relationship in which the husband and wife lead separate social lives, communicate infrequently and spend the majority of their lives apart. And yet couples like this have been interviewed and have claimed to be very happily married. In other words, that sort of marriage suits them and their own highly individual needs.

In evaluating whether or not a marriage is satisfactory it is difficult to see how one can do other than rely upon the judgment of the two people most intimately involved. Too many prescriptions exist for "the happy marriage," provided by people who only have the right to talk about what is necessary to make marriage successful for *them*.

Nevertheless, while there can always be disagreement concerning the amount of masked breakdown of marriages, there can be no denial of the increase in visible breakdown. Between 1715 and 1852 the average number of divorces in Great Britain each year was less than two. By 1931, it was 0.4 per 1000 married couples; in 1951 2.6 per 1000 couples, and by 1971 4.1 per 1000 couples. Much of this increase is undoubtedly due to the fact that divorce is easier and cheaper, and a larger proportion of the adult population is marrying than ever before. However, there are other reasons.

MAN CANNOT MARRY FOR BREAD ALONE

Part of the increasing divorce rate can be attributed to the changing attitudes toward marriage. Traditionally, marriage was viewed as an economic arrangement, which provided a certain status and security for both husband and wife, and which sanctioned the bearing and rearing of children who could inherit the family wealth. In this type of marriage the roles of husband and wife were clearly differentiated. Increasingly in this century, the satisfaction of economic needs has been taken for granted and the emphasis has been directed toward fulfillment in terms of personal needs. A British survey of sex and marriage, compiled in 1970 by Geoffrey Gorer[1] reveals the importance attached by married couples to companionship, discussion, sharing activities and interests, trust and understanding. The demands that each partner makes for some measure of emotional fulfillment are becoming increasingly complex, and the opportunity for a wide range of kin to help satisfy those needs has been almost totally lost by the arrival of the nuclear family. Marriage is now expected to provide so much in the way of need fulfillment that it is hardly surprising if it sometimes fails to live up to expectations.

1. *Sex and Marriage in England Today*, Humanities Press, New York, 1971.

ARE YOU OLD ENOUGH FOR MARRIAGE?

The divorce rate is about twice as high for women who marry before they are twenty years old, compared to those between the ages of twenty and twenty-four. These marriages are particularly at risk if the couple marry because of pre-marital conception or if the marriage proves to be infertile.

As a growing number of couples are marrying when one or both partners is below the age of twenty this is one of the factors which has undoubtedly increased the incidence of visible marital breakdown. The earlier a person marries, the greater the chances of one or both partners' needs changing to such an extent that intolerable pressures are put on the relationship. It is also worth bearing in mind that, as long as life expectancy continues to increase, so does the average length of a lifelong marriage. In 1911, "till death us do part" meant, on average, twenty-eight years; in 1967, forty-two years.

Reasons for marital breakdown tend to depend not only on the age of the partners at marriage but also on the "age" of the marriage itself. The British statistics showing the percentage of divorces according to the duration of the marriage are striking in that one in five of the marriages ending in divorce has, in fact, lasted twenty years or more (even if masked breakdown has actually taken place some years previously). A marriage which has "lasted" fifteen or twenty years breaks down for very different reasons from those of a marriage which ends after a year.

Marriages can be broadly divided into at least three phases. The first stage spans approximately the initial five years of marriage, during which breakdown is the result of failure to establish the necessary minimum physical and emotional relationship. Marriages which negotiate this phase with reasonable success enter a second phase during which the couple may have to cope with adjusting to a broadened family life involving children, often the nonemployed wife and mother and the changing needs of both partners. The third phase, starting after about twenty years of marriage, typically sees the children leaving home, the wife taking up some form of employment and coping with menopausal problems, and the husband coping with his own emotional form of menopause involving a compromise with his early career aspirations and awareness of encroaching age. From the statistics it is clear that 14 percent fail at the first hurdle, a further 53 percent or more fail to negotiate the second phase, and 33 percent of marriages fail after fifteen years or more.

HOW IMPORTANT ARE ENGAGEMENTS?

While not in itself a cause of breakdown, the period of engagement, whether formalized or not, has been found by social scientists to be the best single predictor of marital success. Unhappy engagements often result in unhappy marriages and happy engagements in happy marriages. The shorter the period of acquaintance before marriage, the greater the likelihood of marital breakdown.

Dominian,[2] summarizing a number of research studies, suggests that at least nine months of engagement provide an average probability of success. It would not be fair to say that short engagements are doomed; they are merely severely handicapped, because so much is left to chance. Elopement also appears to be inadvisable. One study[3] has found that, whereas between 80 and 90 percent of all marriages in Western society are "successful," only 48 percent of elopements are.

Unfortunately, prolonged engagements cannot guarantee marital satisfaction. The comment of one unhappily married woman who had courted for four years is probably painfully

2. J. Dominian, *Marital Breakdown,* Penguin Books, New York, 1968.
3. P. Popenoe, "A Study of 738 Elopements," *American Sociological Review* (1938), 3.

true in many cases: "I don't think it matters how long you wait because you are blind to the things you don't want to see anyway."

TO BED OR NOT TO BED?

Many people believe that sexual compatibility is all-important. Most research indicates that, contrary to some people's expectations, sexual compatibility is not the key to marital happiness. There are many happy couples who, by any definition, have a poor sex life. The wife rarely experiences orgasm, or the husband is impotent, or both fail to achieve satisfactory orgasms. On the other hand, there are couples whose only periods of harmony occur in bed. More important than sexual compatibility is psychological compatibility. Couples who are psychologically well matched are likely to show a surprising degree of tolerance for the unsatisfactory areas of their sexual relationship. The psychologically ill-matched couples show no such tolerance, but instead are prone to exaggerate their sexual difficulties. The position is not helped by the obsession with being normal or, preferably, slightly above normal in one's sexual drives and accomplishments. The national average may be two acts of intercourse a week, some people are only satisfied with two daily, while others are content to let weeks pass without intercourse.

However, research does suggest a relationship between the quality of marriage and the wife's sexual response. One study showed that in a sample of 8000 women, only 4.4 percent of the very happily married wives did not experience orgasm, compared with 19 percent of the unhappily married group. It would be misleading to suggest that happiness in marriage is always related to the number of orgasms experienced by the woman, or that frequency of orgasm is always related to sexual satisfaction (one can be experienced without the other). Evidence suggests that a wife is more likely to have positive feelings about her sex life if she and her husband are closely involved with each other's activities. Since the wife's interest in sex often tends to depend more heavily on a sense of interpersonal closeness, it is difficult for her to find gratification in sex in the context of highly segregated marital roles.

The question which remains open to controversy is whether premarital sexual experience affects marital relations. The Kinsey Report claimed that those experiencing orgasm before marriage were more likely to experience it after marriage. However, more recent studies refute this finding. To the extent that knowing a person well involves knowing him or her physically and sexually, premarital intercourse between engaged people must broaden their understanding of each other and hence enhance their chances of a successful marital relationship. One husband summed up the irony of the situation: "After we married, we both wished desperately that we had not slept with anybody else. Yet the worst thing possible would be to marry somebody just because you wanted sexual intercourse. Until you've got over the sex hangup you can't start to get to know a person."

DO CHILDREN HELP A MARRIAGE?

Some 27 percent of divorces involve no children, although only 9 percent of marriages are childless. One must allow for the fact that often children have grown up before their parents divorce (and hence the parents come into the "childless" category), but childless marriages always appear more prone to visible breakdown, especially if this is a result of a lack of desire for children. This may be because of the temperament of childless couples, but will also reflect the general unwillingness of a responsible couple to have children if they feel that their marriage is under stress. There is also little need to stay together if there are no children affected. There is probably a good deal more masked breakdown in marriages with children, where the couple keep up a front "for the sake of the children."

How far do children actually contribute to marital breakdown? It is possible to make a tentative generalization, based on the comments of many married parents. Almost without exception, they felt that children enhanced an already strong marriage but probably dealt the final blow to a marriage built on a shaky foundation. Peter de Vries said that "The value of marriage is not that adults produce children but that children produce adults."

LIKE FATHER, LIKE SON

Much has been written about the *invisibility* of married life in Western society. This is revealed by the shock felt at the divorce of close friends who were thought to be ideally suited. One tends to hear little of a couple's real marital problems. Indeed, people are often unaware of some of the problems in their own parents' marriage. Research shows that in deciding what sort of a man she wants, a woman's preference will undoubtedly be influenced by her parents and their marriage. The one proven way for parents to help their daughter toward a happy marriage is for their relationship to be a happy one. She will then expect marriage to be happy. When problems do occur in her own marriage she will be more likely to feel that they can be worked out, because she will have seen her parents do this. If she respects her father and the qualities he represents, she will be better inclined toward men generally. This in turn will mean that men will probably respond more positively to her. If she does not approve of one or both of her parents, or their marriage, the advice must be that no marriage needs to be identical to any other. It is important to work out what feels right to the two people involved, however weird others may think their behavior.

Enough is now known about the importance of childhood

experiences in forming lifelong attitudes for us to examine the social background factors specifically related to marital success. A well-known study of 450 married and divorced couples[4] claims that the background circumstances most predictive of lasting marital happiness are, in order of importance, as follows:

1. Happiness of parents' marriage.
2. Childhood happiness.
3. Lack of conflict with mother.
4. Firm, but not harsh, home discipline.
5. Strong attachment to mother.
6. Strong attachment to father.
7. Lack of conflict with father.
8. Parental frankness about sex.
9. Infrequency and mildness of childhood punishments.
10. Premarital attitudes to sex, free from disgust or aversion.

DOES SOCIAL CLASS MATTER?

The statistics on marriages between people from different social backgrounds are not heartening in terms of success rates. Neither are such marriages as numerous as people might think. "Like" really does tend to marry "like," especially when the similarity is one of social background. For example, in Britain only 10 percent of all marriages cross the social class barriers.

Where cross-class marriages do occur, marital problems are clearly more severe and more frequent than usual. American and British studies have demonstrated a strong relationship between a common social class background and marital adjustment. The problems are obvious. Each partner brings a set of totally different and often severely opposing expecta-

4. Lewis M. Terman, *Psychological Factors in Marital Happiness*, Mc-Graw-Hill Book Co., New York, 1938.

tions to the marriage. In many traditional working-class communities husbands and wives lead psychologically independent lives. Each is clear about his own role; there is little overlap and little sharing of a common life except briefly in bed. Husband and wife converse little with each other. Their parental roles, too, are clearly defined: the father is authoritarian, the mother supportive. The man leads a social life from which women are excluded, and the woman has her own social arrangements to which men are not invited. This is in contrast to the typical middle-class family where the stress is put on the mutual enjoyment of doing things together, participatory decision making and psychological intimacy. There are common responsibilities in child rearing and an increasing emphasis on both partners leading independent lives outside the home.

Where cross-class marriages do occur, it is usually the woman who marries "upward," and the marriage stands a better chance of success if this is the case. Why should adjustment be smoother when it is the male partner who has the higher status? Research into marital adjustment provides one possible answer. Even in an age of apparently increasing sexual equality, the major adjustment—and in many cases almost the entire adjustment—is made by the wife. Since an upward shift in social class is often more rewarding both economically and socially than a downward shift, one would expect less stress in those cases where the wife moved upward than in those where she was expected to shift her values downward.

ARE SOME PEOPLE BETTER SUITED TO MARRIAGE?

Undoubtedly some people are a better "marriage bet" than others. Certain characteristics have been clearly shown to be related to marital success. This is not to say that there are individuals who can never be part of a happy marriage, but for some people marriage will require more energetic adjustment. Probably the chances of marital happiness will depend as much on the ability of the partner to tolerate or compensate for the individual's weaknesses as on his own ability to change.

There are three personality characteristics which have been shown, either singly or in combination with each other, to be particularly associated with marital breakdown. If either partner is lacking in self-esteem this creates difficulties—the problem with people who have a poor opinion of themselves is that they tend to have a poor opinion of others, including their partners. It is difficult to love someone else if one does not already love oneself. Second, people who have failed to achieve a minimum of emotional independence from their parents and spouse are also likely to have unhappy marriages because they may be unable to make mature relationships of their own. In addition, visible or masked deprivation of parental warmth and love can bring to a marriage a number of unresolved problems related to the need for security and fear of giving affection openly. One study[5] summarized the characteristics of happily and unhappily married people. The happily married were emotionally stable, considerate of others, yielding, companionable, self-confident and emotionally dependent. In contrast the unhappily married tended to be emotionally unstable, critical of others, dominating, isolated, lacking in self-confidence and emotionally self-sufficient.

MYTHS ABOUT MARRIAGE

Myths about the factors that are likely to help or hinder a marriage prevail in abundance—and will probably continue to do so as long as people believe that they are victims of a situation which they do not always understand and often

5. E. W. Burgess and P. Wallin, *Engagement and Marriage*, J. P. Lippincott, Chicago, 1953.

cannot control. When we know that there are certain factors which contribute to marital success and others which limit the chances, it is not helpful to find that the situation has been confused by a web of myths entangling the fact.

"You Will Recognize Mr. Right as Soon as He Comes Along"

The mass media, particularly when aimed at the teenage market, actively reinforce the notion of "love at first sight." It is the stuff of which teenage dreams are made, not to mention the dreams of the advertising executive. But evidence suggests that permanent relationships are not normally founded on that basis.

In one American research study[6] involving 1000 engaged and 666 married couples, respondents were asked how soon they had felt a strong physical attraction for each other. Only 17 percent of men and 15 percent of women replied "immediately" or "within one or two days." About 50 percent of the men and 58 percent of the women said that strong physical attraction developed two months or longer after their first meeting.

"May-December Marriages Don't Work"

The problems aroused by large age differences between husband and wife have been thoroughly explored in novels and films. "Older woman–younger man" marriages have more problems than "older man–younger woman" ones, probably partly because they are less acceptable to society. People tend to view a "cradle snatcher" more critically than a "sugar daddy." But overall, large age differences do not appear to affect marital stability to any significant extent. A large American study[7] showed that the happiest wives were those who were from four to ten years older than their husbands; the

6. *Ibid.*
7. *Ibid.*

happiest husbands had wives who were twelve or more years younger.

"Mixed Marriages Are Doomed to Failure"
There are many people who still think that mixed marriages are "not natural." We have already seen how genuine differences in social background and future expectations place extra stress on a marriage between people of different social classes. The same can be said of marriages incorporating more than one race or religion. Research shows that marriages between Catholics and Protestants encounter more difficulties than do those between members of the same faith, with a greater subsequent rate of breakdown. Surprisingly, however, interracial marriages have a significantly higher success rate than interreligious ones. There has been recent evidence to suggest that black-white marriages, if anything, are even stronger than average. This probably reflects the tremendous determination to succeed against all odds that characterizes so many interracial marriages.

A mixed marriage is by no means doomed. It is important that the two partners are aware of their differences and have come to terms with the reality of the situation as far as possible before marriage. However much the couple is determined to make a success of their marriage, their parents may not provide much encouragement. And problems are often at their severest when children first arrive. But if the hurdles are higher in a mixed marriage, the potential rewards may often be greater. Individual differences can make for variety and excitement in what might otherwise have been a monochrome relationship.

"If You Can't Make Your First Marriage Work, You Can't Expect Your Second Marriage to Work Either"
There is considerable argument over the facts about remarriage and its chances of success. The controversy usually re-

volves around the definition of marital success. Few people would suggest that marriages are successful as long as they do not end in divorce. However, statistics for divorce and remarriage are more detailed than they are for other areas of breakdown (for instance where people continue to live together, but unhappily so) and do serve as an indication of marital breakdown.

If one or both partners have been divorced once, then a marriage is twice as likely to break down as one where neither partner has been married before. As for men, the chances of successful remarriage are slightly less than for women. However, the picture is brighter when one compares previous and present marriages of divorcees. That is to say, *their* divorce rate for first marriage was 100 percent. In comparison, a subsequent divorce rate of 35 percent is a vast improvement.

It is important to bear a number of points in mind when considering divorce statistics. Some studies suggest that certain people are "divorce-prone." It is only fair to point out that these people are not necessarily excessively neurotic. They may simply have overcome the taboo that society places on divorce. Once they have rejected the social norm that pressures people into staying married for a lifetime, it will be easier to do the same again, with each subsequent marriage. Some people may be unwilling to accept a second-rate relationship. If this is the case, their chances of breakdown will be greater, but a subsequent marriage which does "last" will probably be richer and more satisfying than other mediocre ones which appear to undergo no difficulties.

MATE SELECTION AND MARITAL SUCCESS

If we were asked what the most basic cause of marital breakdown was, with no hesitation our answer would refer to faulty mate selection—faulty in that present choice may not coincide with future needs. For those experiencing marital breakdown, this may sound too simple to be mentioned. But evidently it is not as obvious as it seems. There may be more to be learned from one's attitude to choosing a partner than from the weaknesses of the marriage itself. This is apparent from the answers divorcees give when asked what they have learned from their first marriage. A large proportion reply, "We should never have married in the first place" or "If I had known what I know now I would never have married" or "I thought it would all work out okay once we were married."

What is it that goes wrong at the courtship stage? We must first look at the functions of courtship. To begin with, dating is a form of "window shopping," with no obligation to buy the merchandise on display. It is simply a popular form of recreation with other perquisites, such as the increased status a teenager achieves if he dates a physically attractive member of the opposite sex.

Dating has increasingly long-term implications, however. It provides men and women with the opportunity to associate with each other. This serves to eliminate some of the mystery that surrounds the opposite sex (a mystery well nurtured by the relatively small families of Western society, where many children grow up with no siblings of the opposite sex). Dating allows a person to discover something about who he is. He may learn about the way others respond to his personality —what it is that attracts or repels them. He may also learn to understand about the personalities of others, so that he can gradually start to recognize the qualities in others that he particularly likes and the sort of people whom he most warms to. This process of learning by trial and error eventually narrows down his field of eligible partners (either on a lighthearted, uncommitted basis or with a serious view to marriage).

Eventually, dating assumes rather more serious implications when it becomes courtship (here defined as dating of a more permanent and committed nature). But the functions previously outlined are not as irrelevant or as hedonistic as they might seem. Without a long period of uncommitted dating, involving relationships with people of many types, an individual would find it difficult to choose a permanent partner on realistic grounds.

After the field of eligibles has been considerably narrowed down, on the bases of personality, background and availability, a more or less definite decision can be made. At this point courtship (and for many people, engagement) assumes its final function: it provides the opportunity for two committed people to get to know each other better, to outline their plans for the future, to discover what they expect from each other in their marriage and what they expect from marriage itself. Increasingly, they will project themselves into the roles of husband and wife (or perhaps even father and mother), rather than boyfriend and girlfriend.

William Congreve, the eighteenth-century playwright, defined courtship as "a very witty prologue to a very dull play." How far *is* courtship a rather unrealistic, overglamorized prelude to a lifetime of monotony? For many people, the stereotyped courtship pattern is summed up by the American sociologist Winch's definition of dating as "a situation of erotically-tinged, fun-oriented recreation." And yet undoubtedly one of the functions of courtship is to test out one's choice of partner (and indeed to test out oneself) in an attempt to ensure that both individuals are suited to each other and to marriage. Obviously, if this is the case, the more closely the premarital relationship can approximate the marital one, the more realistic will be the assessment of the chances of marital success. Many people are against "trial marriage" in the form of living together, for moral reasons. It is certainly not for anyone else to force a couple into a particular way of life. The advantage of actually living together (and not just spending the occasional night together), however, is that the couple experience something close to the "dailiness" of married life. If a relationship is based on dinner by candlelight every Friday night it is difficult to imagine what it might be like to wake up together on a Monday morning, in a rush for work. The data one has, with which to assess the relationship, are extremely limited in such a situation. Your fiancée may look immaculate across the dining table with her flicked-up hair and newly polished nails. But you always swore that you could never sleep next to an eyeful of curlers and what you have yet to learn is that she refuses to do any housework for fear of spoiling her nails.

So much of marriage is based on what sociologists call "task-oriented" activities—tasks such as budgeting, housekeeping and child bearing and rearing—that a courtship based on occasional dates is bound to be a rather inefficient way of preparing a couple for what lies ahead. Far from being a period of uninterrupted bliss, courtship is a time of adjustment when stress and a certain amount of conflict and compromise are inevitable. Some of the stresses of engagement are peculiar to engagement itself (such as being separated from each other for what may seem to be long periods of time). It is important, however, to be aware of the areas of stress that have implications for the marriage itself.

The earlier the danger signals—the potential sources of conflict—are spotted, the sooner adjustments can be made. Early compromise and adjustment are less likely to cause resentment. It is only too easy for bad habits to creep into a relationship unnoticed and extremely difficult to eliminate them after years of use. Courtship is the stage to learn about your own and each other's strengths and weaknesses and the time to either resolve differences or admit that compromise is impossible—before it is too late.

Many people suffering from an unhappy marriage have asked themselves, "Where did I go wrong?" . . . "Where did I make my mistake?" To introduce blame to explain an unsatisfactory relationship is not helpful, and the notion that someone, at some time, has "made a mistake" can be misleading. For a start, it has been said that "the man who makes no mistakes does not usually make anything" and this is probably nowhere more true than in the marriage stakes. Marriage is always a gamble to some extent. No one can realistically bank on the success of marriage. Like all major risks, it offers the gambler the possibility of major rewards as well as major losses. Fortunately, even if one does "lose" and one's marriage breaks down, there is bound to be something to be learned from the experience.

In short, people may make a variety of mistakes, but so-called "mistakes" are more likely to be a conflict of needs than severe character faults. For example, the woman who wants to describe every detail of her day, including increased food prices and how long her washing took to dry, would drive some men mad. Others would be bored to distraction by a quiet introverted female who kept her feelings bottled up and liked to spend her evenings reading in silence. There are few qualities that everyone would evaluate in the same way. Take a street of ordinary houses, all looking pretty much the same. In one, Mary says, "I like a man to be a man . . . he's entitled to his evening out with the boys . . . who wants to see a man with an apron around his waist . . . ?" Next door, Jean says, "We both work hard all day, so why should it be me who cooks the evening meal *and* washes up? . . . I like a man who pulls his weight around the house and is not afraid that he's a sissy when he makes the bed." Farther up the same road, Pat is complaining to her friends that her husband is "over-sexed." Her neighbor, Gloria is worried because her husband seems to have "lost interest" in her. In fact, *both* husbands expect to make love about twice a week; it is the *wives'* needs that differ. Pat thinks, "Once a month is quite enough to satisfy any decent man." Gloria thinks making love is a bit like cleaning your teeth—it should be done every night without question, and preferably in the morning as well.

Once it becomes clear that people's expectations can vary so considerably, it is obviously impossible to talk about outright mistakes. It is more useful to look at a broken marriage in terms of incompatibility of needs. Indeed, this new approach now has legal backing. Recent divorce laws have abandoned the idea of sin by one guilty party and examined rocking marriages in terms of "irreconcilable breakdown." Nevertheless, it would be naïve to suggest that people are faultless or that they cannot learn from their mistakes in choosing a partner. There must be something to be learned from a broken marriage. If marriages can dissolve without anyone being "to blame," how can one ensure that it does not happen again?

"Mistakes" in mate selection are of two basic types:

1. Conflicts which emerge after the couple have "committed themselves to each other" because large areas of the relationship have been left unexplored. The couple thought they knew each other better than they really did. Obviously, a couple is more likely to lay themselves open to this problem if they marry too quickly.
2. Conflicts which are recognized by the two people involved, but which they find impossible to satisfactorily resolve.

I *UNKNOWN CONFLICTS*

If two people marry before knowing each other extremely well, they may be dismayed by the revelations of their partner when it is too late to reconsider their choice. Mark and Elizabeth were such a couple.

They married in a haze of champagne and candlelight after a courtship of three weeks. They felt they had gotten to know each other so well that nothing about one another could ever surprise them, so much so that they had not even bothered to check up on certain crucial plans. Their marriage never really recovered from the shock its shaky foundations received two weeks after the honeymoon. Mark had automatically assumed that his wife's well-established career would take second place for a few years while they reared a family. Elizabeth had no intention of jeopardizing a highly lucrative career by opting out for several years. In any case, she disliked children. This presented a situation in which any compromise was bound to be unsatisfactory. Child rearing is a highly demanding job for the most maternal of women, without thrusting it upon an unwilling one. Mark felt he could not tolerate the prospect of a life without children and the marriage ended in divorce. But neither fell into the same trap again.

Another danger of marrying before a relationship has been explored in depth is that a whirlwind courtship may leave the couple on the crest of a wave of elation. The reality of the mood swings that most people are prone to may come as a shock once the couple are thrown into the "dailiness" of marriage. In short, it is probably worth asking yourself, "Have I seen my partner in situations of stress?" and, "Can I cope with the way he reacts to stress?" if you are not to be disillusioned by severe mood swings or prolonged bouts of sulking or depression after marriage.

What you agree on is easy. Find out what you disagree on, what his demands will be, and what he will do if you don't meet them. You don't really know him until you've seen him angry.
Eric Berne[8]

---

8. *Sex in Human Loving,* Simon and Schuster, New York, 1970.

Once an individual asks himself, "Am I ready for marriage?" his answers to a number of questions will be a useful indicator of his "marriageability."[9]

1. *Know Yourself:* this is probably even more important than knowing your partner because it indicates the degree to which you will be able to adapt to another individual's demands.

a. Can you list your best points? What do you have to contribute to a marriage?
b. Can you list your worst points? What might hinder your relationship?
c. Would your partner agree with your answers?

2. *Know Your Partner:* even though you may be head-over-heels in love, it should be possible for you to realistically assess your partner's assets and faults, without feeling the urge to change the latter. If you believe, like G. K. Chesterton, that "A man's friend likes him but leaves him as he is: his wife loves him and is always trying to turn him into somebody else" then this could have serious consequences for your marriage. If you really want to change him, you should not be considering marriage to him in the first place. Hopefully you fell in love with a human being, not an idealized image of one.

a. What are your partner's best qualities?
b. What are your partner's worst qualities?
c. Would he/she agree with you?
d. Are you sure you can live with his faults? If he has habits which annoy you even in the flushes of early love, beware; they will probably annoy you even more in a few years' time.

9. The exercises earlier in this book should help people to answer these questions.

3. *Define Your Needs:*

a. What are your own needs in marriage?
b. What are the needs your partner expects to have satisfied by you?
c. Will you both be able to satisfy these needs?
d. How will you come to terms with not being able to satisfy each other's needs, if the situation arises?

4. *Define the Facts of Marriage Itself:*

a. Can you list what you expect to be the best things about your marriage?
b. What will be the worst things about your marriage (either within your control, like bad temper, or out of your control, such as feeling obliged to go out to work) ?

Only when these questions have been answered can one examine the extent to which both partners "match" one another in terms of finding themselves complementary.

II *KNOWN BUT UNRESOLVABLE CONFLICTS*

For many couples it is not the inability to answer the questions that raises problems but the content of the answers themselves.

The majority of pitfalls of marriage can be gathered under the blanket term of "bad habits," whether these are seemingly trivial personal habits such as making love with one's socks on or slurping one's soup, or more fundamental ones such as a lazy style of communication.

There will be many indicators for the future, long before the couple reaches the altar. Read the signs. If your fiancé likes three nights out a week with the boys and downs six beers a night, he could want more nights and more beers once

he is your husband. If you feel that your fiancée nags un-
necessarily, how much more intolerable her nagging will be
when you are actually married to her. *Never, ever* think that
you can change your partner once you are married. It is not
fair to your partner and you probably will not succeed anyway. But you will succeed in annoying him. If there are characteristics that you would like to change in your partner, you
must discuss the matter before you marry. If you long to
marry a certain man but feel that you cannot live with his
quick temper, you must make your feelings clear. It is then up
to both of you to resolve the problem before you marry.
Either he can learn to control his temper or you must learn to
accept it as one of his faults. In most cases it is probably up to
both individuals to change, in the sense of learning to tolerate
each other's weaknesses without allowing them to jeopardize
the relationship.

Bad habits are also the cause of much sexual dissatisfaction.
This is less likely to emerge as a problem during courtship
but it is good to be aware of the need for vitality in love making. Husbands complain that their wives have "let themselves
go" since marriage or that they show no spirit during love
making. Wives retaliate with complaints that they are "left
cold" by their husbands' advances. Many men fail to realize
that foreplay is far more important for a woman's ultimate
satisfaction than it is for a man's. Wives talk of wanting to be
"seduced" again as they were when they were being courted. It
is essential to avoid sexual monotony. A new position in love
making or a session on the living-room rug has revitalized
many a flagging pair of lovers.

It is also worth the potential spouse asking himself why he
is considering marriage. Many people feel a pressure to con-
form when they reach a certain age and all their peers seem
to be heading for the altar. It is important that you should
feel that you cannot visualize life without the person you are
set on marrying. Obviously, it is acceptable to be enthusiastic

about the idea of marriage in itself, but people who feel that way should probably examine their motives very carefully and make sure that they are not in love only with the idea of marriage.

A "good" marriage results from finding the right sort of person at the right time. It is certainly possible to find the right partner but not be ready for the demands of married life. Unfortunately, it is also only too easy to be ready for marriage but to be unable to find the right spouse. The danger here is that a person may convince himself he is in love with a person when he is only in love with the notion of being in love. The qualities of the individual he chooses are relatively unimportant.

Keith fell into this trap. He enjoyed the ritual "courting" of a girl in the traditional sense. Either she was rejected after the first date (usually on the basis of physical appearance) or he immediately perceived her as a potential wife and wooed her with flowers, chocolates and hints of marriage. Most girls were eventually scared off by this approach. He was totally unable to enjoy an evening out with a girl for its own sake, because she was good company to be with. Keith was in love with the idea of romance, as perpetuated by television advertisements and short stories in women's magazines. Unfortunately, he met Andrea, who was equally taken with the idea of marriage, but for different reasons. Andrea could not wait for her wedding day when she would be the center of attention and look radiantly beautiful on the arm of her Prince Charming. It never occurred to her that marriage and a wedding day were not the same thing. Consequently, when Keith and Andrea gratefully plunged into marriage the effects were disastrous: Keith was quickly disenchanted with a woman who did not always look "dressed to kill." Andrea was peeved when her wedding ring—like her marriage—began to grow dull after too many dishes. Andrea may well have voiced the cynical words of Thornton Wilder who said,

"Marriage is a bribe to make a housekeeper think she's a householder."

Thus, one can talk about the wrong reasons for marrying, even though such marriages do not always end disastrously.

Robert lived with his mother, a widow, until he was thirty. He was desperate for some independence as she insisted on treating him like a boy of sixteen. She made him feel inhibited with girls and when he finally did meet a girl who liked him he proposed within a month. They were separated after a year of marriage. He had married for an immature reason—the desire to escape from a domineering mother. Unfortunately, having lived with his doting mother for so long, he found the "give and take" necessary in married life very difficult to accept. He expected everything to be done for him, domestically, and his wife felt that she was taken for granted. His mother constantly told him that his bride was not good enough for him and he felt torn between the two women. Robert was quite obviously extremely immature both in his selfishness and in his ignorance of the facts of married life.

People who have never had to look after themselves are likely to find it difficult to adjust to marriage. They have never undertaken the domestic tasks of cooking, cleaning, laundering, budgeting and being totally responsible for their own way of life. Many wives report that their husbands are far more appreciative of what is done for them at home if their bachelor existence involved some of the same tasks. They are also often more willing to share the domestic chores.

If suitability for marriage is based on maturity, can an immature person be part of a happy marriage? The answer is probably an affirmative one. But the crucial factor will be the other partner.

Bill wanted to marry Peggy in spite of the fact that he knew she was selfish, egotistical and spoiled by her mother and a large family of older siblings. However, he loved her enough to accept her shortcomings because he enjoyed her company and could not envisage life without her. Friends who knew Peggy said he must be mad.

One must accept the fact, however, that he reached his decision through a mature assessment of the facts. He knew that marriage for him would involve more "giving" than "taking." Perhaps the crucial factor in the success of this marriage was Bill's maturity. He had been the eldest son of a widowed mother with six children. It therefore came naturally to him to fend for himself and to invest more energy in caring for others than expecting others to look after him. It would probably be fair to assume that the chances of *two* immature people making a successful marriage are almost nil, because they would both make unacceptable and incompatible demands on each other.

It is important for observers of a marriage to remember that needs are only incompatible if they are so perceived by the two people directly experiencing the marriage. It is only too easy for onlookers to assume that everyone else feels the same way and has the same needs as they do. Take the case of "infidelity," for example. If a fiancé finds it difficult to remain sexually faithful during engagement, he will probably find it impossible after marriage. But what is generally assumed to be a "weakness" is only a danger signal in courtship if the partner on the receiving end finds the behavior intolerable to live with. In other words, if both partners are quite clear that they need a variety of sexual partners to be happy and can accept this need in each other then the situation, if rather unusual, by no means bodes ill for the future.

TWOGETHERNESS OR TOGETHERNESS?

"Like fingerprints, all marriages are different." George Bernard Shaw's comment reflects the difficulty of assessing the minimum requirements for a marriage to survive. One wonders how one's closest friend tolerates the atrocities her partner deals her; she would rather suffer his faults than do without his strengths. And she balks at the prospect of enduring a husband as steady as one's own.

But survival is not the be-all and end-all of marriage. How many people would opt for a number of happy years with a variety of husbands, even if each marriage ended in divorce, rather than a lifetime of frustration with one outsize bore? Many, we hope. This is by no means an attempt to belittle the devastating effects of a divorce on a married couple and "significant others," merely a plea not always to accept second best. However, a change in one or both partners does not always denote the end of a marriage. Indeed, it is the lifeblood for some. One happily married man summed up his marital requirements as "a unique opportunity for learning to handle and welcome change, in an atmosphere of trust and acceptance, while maintaining a consistent thread of sameness in a world where there is less and less sameness from one year to the next." And it was one extremely disenchanted husband who said, "Nothing's changed between us. I haven't been surprised by her in eleven years of marriage."

Many people are quick to assume that a permanent relationship has no alternative but to deteriorate. The writer Arnold Bennett said that the horror of marriage lies in its "dailiness." All acuteness of a relationship is rubbed away by this. And yet it is this very routine that can promote the emotional security sought by so many. It is important for people to realize that familiarity need not breed contempt, but that it must be expected to breed a feeling of being comfortable, and this feeling does not occur in peaks. There is nothing wrong with habit as long as it does not give rise to boredom and as long as it does not prevent the moments of romantic intensity which should still be possible in a long-standing relationship. The danger of routine is that it may cause either of the partners to take the other too much for granted and so induce monotony which may preclude the level of intensity vital to a relationship.

Perhaps the real danger of "dailiness" is that partners may not realize that marriage does not endure because it remains the same. It is more likely to last for the very reason that it is a constantly changing way of life, making incredibly high demands on those involved.

There is no reason to presume that with time love need fade in either quality or quantity. Its intensity may simply mellow. And often the most striking difference between happily and unhappily married couples is not their *love* but their *liking* for each other. One wife, unhappy enough to be considering separation, said, "I'm still in love with my husband . . . he still attracts me a lot. But this does not mean I enjoy living with him. In fact he's not a nice person. If he was married to one of my friends I would not like him at all." In contrast, a wife who felt her marriage was "tremendous" thought that the best thing about it was that her husband was her "best friend."

The notion of "togetherness"—a combination of friendship, the sharing of good and bad periods and a certain invulnerability to the rest of the world—is the quality most often stressed by happily married couples. This would appear to be in direct opposition to our emphasis on personal growth in a context of individual freedom and independence. It is our aim to demonstrate that no one need choose between the two. One's potential for growth is not diminished by "togetherness."

However, "togetherness" is a term which smacks of sweet people living in a candyfloss world—a quality designed to cause emotional indigestion and nausea. We are referring to the experience of encountering life together. The experience of any event will be unique to each partner. But the presence of the other allows for amplification of the experience. In this way, two people can live and develop *through* one another rather than *in spite of* one another. They do run the risk of growing apart. But this risk is greater for couples who do not share their experiences, for they will change anyway and their partner will have no opportunity to incorporate this change into his perception of their relationship. Encountering life together does not mean doing everything as a couple. A unisex couple who dress, look, talk and live alike are not developing through one another. They represent two people acting as one to provide the strength and security that neither feels alone. They have yet to reach the stage of exploring life as individuals, with the confidence in their partner to enable them to branch out from a secure base.

Perhaps the danger is to perceive marriage as a "funnel" whereby the original breadth of each person's experience is whittled down until the ultimate convergence produces what Henry Fielding has described as "that monstrous animal, a husband and wife." It may be more heartening to view marriage as a megaphone, of which both partners share the same mouthpiece. The product which emerges from the other end is far greater than the sum of the contributions made by the two partners.

9·The Exploding Marriage

"Marriage is dead."

Female university student, 1972

"A wedding ring is a small band of gold that cuts off your circulation."

Anon

"The trouble with marriage is that it restricts the people involved. It swaps security for coercion, and freedom for fear of loneliness."

Housewife, 1972

"Marriage will probably only last another generation. When babies can be created artificially there will be no necessity for the family as we know it."

Male doctor, 1972

"Family life will increasingly be organised around marriage, rather than around parenthood, and the marital relationship will become both more important to the well-being of participants and more fragile."

R. S. Weiss[1]

1. "Marriage and the Family in the Near Future," Katherine Elliot (Ed.), *The Family and Its Future*, Churchill, 1970.

"Marriage is essentially an ongoing encounter with growth. We can grow as individuals throughout our lives if we desire, and marriage can be a relationship that will facilitate this growth for both husband and wife."

Herbert Otto[2]

Magazines and newspapers every week seem to carry some new revelations on the "state of the union" in our age of transience. Pundits speculate over whether marriage will survive, and if so in what form. Bulletins are "posted" periodically on the health of the old institution. Our thesis is that, in its traditional form, marriage *is* dying, dissolving, disintegrating. But the explosion does not mean automatic destruction. The more dramatic the explosion, the greater the number of fragments remaining. Some people suggest that we pick up those pieces and incorporate them into a new form of marriage. Others wish to discard all those remains and advocate radical alternatives—some of which we will be examining in this chapter. But first, let us examine the institution of marriage—"an institution which simplifies life but complicates living," as Jean Rostand put it. Why have people always joked about marriage being "not a word, but a sentence"?

MARRIAGE—PUBLIC HEALTH PROBLEM NO. 1

One of the consequences of the liberation of women's self-consciousness is that the institution founded on the assumption that they occupy a servile, inferior role is now seen as a major cause of physical and mental ill-health in women. Jessie Bernard[3] estimates that marriage is roughly twice as advantageous to men as it is to women. She shows that the mental

2. *More Joy in Your Marriage*, Hawthorn Books, New York, 1969.
3. *The Future of Marriage*, Bantam, New York, 1973.

health of married men is far better than that of single men. They show fewer symptoms of psychological distress and are only half as likely to commit suicide. The American house-wife, on the other hand, is nine times as likely to attempt suicide as a working woman. Dr. Bernard claims that the characteristic illness of married women today is depression.

It is wives who are driven mad by the anachronistic structure of marriage. The simple truth is that being a housewife makes women sick.

Jessie Bernard[4]

Dr. Bernard's figures show that this means literally sick as well as figuratively sick. Wives suffer much more from anxiety, unhappiness and mental stress than the single woman. 64.5 percent of Boston suicide attempts are by housewives, who mostly try to kill themselves on Mondays or Thursdays at 10 A.M.

It is mostly wives, not husbands, who think about divorce, wives who see problems starting sooner and lasting longer and wives who show less desire to save the marriage.

Jessie Bernard[5]

The "dropout" American wife is becoming an increasingly common phenomenon. Clearly, traditional marriage cannot survive women's liberation.

4. Dr. Bernard in an interview with Jeremy Campbell, *Evening Stand-ard*, April 12, 1972.
5. *Ibid.*

THE FUNCTIONS OF MARRIAGE

The functions of marriage have always been threefold, with the emergence of one addition in the face of contemporary social changes:

1. *Economic:* the setting up of a home.
2. Procreation and rearing of *children.*
3. Satisfaction of *sexual needs* (and the regulation of sexual activity).
4. *Personal growth:* the realization of the personal potential of each partner in the context of an ongoing relationship.

If we examine each of these functions in turn, it will become clear that the basic premises on which they are founded are being laid open to increasing question and doubt. Though the functions themselves are probably not in danger of dying out, so long as marriage itself exists, the rules and regulations, attitudes and expectations, attached to these functions are being forced to change by way of a reflection of other social changes. We will see exactly which societal changes have produced changes in marriage, and the precise direction of those changes.

1. The Economic Function

At one time, partners were almost bound to stay together, particularly where children were involved, because neither could afford to do otherwise. While the woman spent most of her adult life tied to her home by her children, she depended on her husband to provide materially for the family. The cost of divorce rendered it virtually prohibitive for the majority. In any case, alimony nearly crippled many men, and the divorced woman did not have the wherewithal to fend for herself and her offspring.

Not so today. While the shape of income distribution has hardly changed at all, the distribution as a whole has moved upward, with the result that everyone is better off. This has allowed for an increase in individualized activity. People generally use money to buy space. Adult children and grandparents have the opportunity to move elsewhere rather than being forced to double up with the married couple. Divorced women are both better equipped vocationally to find employment if it becomes necessary and better equipped psychologically to cope with that prospect.

Increased affluence is probably one of the few ways in which social changes have actually *improved* the chances of marital success. For many married couples, financial worries are an almost intolerable burden to bear and one which causes friction, often unconsciously, in numerous other areas of interaction.

An increase in the *reliability* of income has emerged on parallel lines with the actual increase in income. This in a sense has resulted in greater geographical mobility, as witnessed by middle-class America and Britain. Once one can ensure economic security almost anywhere, couples feel less tied to their families of origin as a source of security.

2. Child Bearing and Rearing

Seventy years ago, a woman could expect to die a few years after relinquishing her role of mother. Today, by the time the average woman has reached forty, she has few, if any, mothering duties left.[6] At any rate, she has the opportunity to work and the prospect of half her life ahead of her.

Probably the largest recent influence on this aspect of marriage has been the advent of the contraceptive pill. This allows for exact planning of the size and spacing of a family. In fact, the advantages are so far only theoretical for many,

6. Contemporary woman's average life span is seventy-six years compared to fifty-two years in 1901.

because there appears to have been a cultural lag in the adoption of efficient contraceptive methods, especially in the low-income section of the population. Nevertheless, with further contraceptive use, fewer people should experience a "shotgun wedding." Although many of those couples plan to marry anyway, it may impose severe strain on the marriage if young people are forced to marry before they feel ready, because of pregnancy. Research shows that early marriage and child bearing produce lasting economic disabilities. Later marriage should give people the chance to establish themselves (economically, but more important, emotionally) before embarking on parenthood.

The deliberate planning of the number and spacing of children should eventually mean that children are born somewhat later and often in the context of *two* careers. In this situation the woman need not see her adult life consumed by the duties of wife and mother. If marriage is to continue, it is reasonable to predict that the marital, rather than the parental, relationship will become the central core of the family relationship. It has been argued that marriage as an institution does not exist in and for itself, and never has.[7] Marriage is firmly rooted in the family, rather than children being a mere appendage to marriage. This has recently been a subject of much debate and we will discuss later the growing emphasis on establishing a marriage relationship because it is worthwhile in itself.

The role of offspring in marriage can often be to hold together unhappy marriage partners legally, if not under the same roof. The marriage must appear to be kept going "for the sake of the children." Ironically, there is evidence to suggest that many children feel immense relief when their parents do eventually divorce. There is usually less tension involved in living with one parent, and perhaps visiting the

7. Ronald Fletcher, *The Family and Marriage,* Penguin Books Ltd., Harmondsworth, 1962.

other, than in being forced to watch two people crucifying each other.

Nevertheless, divorce can have a devastating effect on the children. Statistically speaking, it is far better for a child to lose a parent through death than divorce (in terms of subsequent behavioral problems, delinquency, suicide, depressive illness and neuroses). Divorce is obviously more difficult to cope with than death in a number of ways. The child may feel guilty: "Have I driven them to this?" Whereas a bereaved child can romanticize the memory of a parent, a child of divorced parents is bound to feel that one parent has been rejected on *some* grounds. In addition, a child is made to feel different from his peers. And he probably has to live with severe rows, and perhaps even physical violence, before the final break is made.

3. The Satisfaction of Sexual Needs

The advent of the contraceptive pill has had one other major influence (apart from regulating reproduction). It has taken the fear out of sex. For the first time ever, both partners can enjoy sex for its own sake, with no fear of unwanted pregnancies. Sexual equality has arrived for many. No longer do women put up with the "animal instincts" of their husbands and suffer in silence; instead they are encouraged and expected to enjoy sex. So great is the need in both partners for the man to sexually satisfy the woman that many people feel that the concept of mutual satisfaction has been taken too far. "The tyranny of the orgasm" is directing our energies away from the variety of pleasures to be had from sexual love.

Many observers of this new phenomenon take a critical view of the ease with which people can now indulge in promiscuity. In fact, people have always indulged in premarital and extramarital sex. The difference is that there is now less fear of talking about it.

4. Personal Growth

We have arrived at the crux of the dilemma, the point at which problems arise because traditional expectations too often cast a shadow over attempts to loosen the marital strait jacket and feel free to be ourselves without in any way rejecting our marital relationship. Not only does the conflict lie between past and present expectations, but between the initial emphasis on romantic feelings at the onset of the relationship and the necessity for learning to live together day-by-day, breakfast after breakfast, and diaper after diaper.

We have already mentioned several significant social changes in passing, including the breakdown of the paternalistic system (where excessive authority is invested in the husband and father), the emergence of woman as a person in her own right, with her growing demands for equality, and the increased value attached to the rights of freedom of action for the individual. Marriage has been pressured into becoming an institution of companionship. The emphasis is on more flexible roles, a more intimate level of communication, the recognition of mutual and conflicting needs and attitudes.

The irony is that, while the sharing and merging of marital roles serve many purposes including equality of the sexes, they raise previously unknown problems. In an autocratic household, the woman has tremendous informal powers. Quite often a household based on outright paternal authority is totally matricentric; day-to-day decisions revolve around the mother. For example, it is by no means unknown for a man not to know where his wife keeps his shirts or to be incapable of making himself a cup of tea because he cannot find the sugar. An apt German saying reflects the reality of the situation, "Der Mann denkt, die Frau lenkt": man proposes, woman disposes. Once the marital roles are less radically differentiated, the husband finds that he has more power in the running of the house, while the woman may have a greater say in major decisions. As for children, they are no longer expected to contribute to the management of the home (and in smaller families, help is not as necessary). But they *are* expected to utilize the opportunities their parents have made available to them for realizing and releasing their potential capabilities, whether these opportunities take the form of theater visits, swimming lessons, building blocks or cake making. From the beginning, the young individual learns that self-realization is a moral requirement although this remains much less so for lower-working-class families whose culture is still geared toward family rather than self-responsibility.[8]

Not only are demands imposed on the child, but parents feel an increasing responsibility, not to mold their children but to allow every possible outlet for self-expression. And as the margin of felt responsibility extends, so does the scope for anxiety about one's children. While children were brought up according to rule-of-thumb custom and tradition, the parental role was far less demanding, for it involved a minimal amount of decision making. In contrast today, the emphasis on producing "individual successes" in a transient, individualistic society, rather than a traditional and repetitious one, offers a vast range of alternative child-rearing methods and the possibility of "failure" never considered before. But, ironically, American children are spending less and less time with their parents (an average of two to three hours over the weekend) and more time with their peers (about six hours on the weekend).[9]

Women, also, are encouraged to "do their own thing," with the result that many are highly educated and hold expectations geared to equality of career in relation to their husbands. But this is liable to cause domestic confusion. If the

8. Basil Bernstein, *Class, Codes and Control,* Vol. 1, Routledge & Kegan Paul, Boston, 1972.
9. Urie Bronfenbrenner.

woman is to work, the husband is almost automatically forced to withdraw some energy from his own specialized work in order to participate in the joint management of home and family.[10] If the husband applies pressure to revert to the more traditional family pattern (where "man's work" and "woman's work" are clearly differentiated and never the twain shall meet) the woman may perceive this as an attack on her vocational identity. Hence the sharing of a vocational and family life undoubtedly generates new tensions and creates potential areas of rivalry and jealousy. Whereas in the traditional family setup, the wife appeared to facilitate the realization of her husband's occupational aims, the sharing pattern may at worst produce a situation in which both partners feel the gains of one are inevitably the losses of the other.

This self-expression within the entire family is bound to result in looser kinship ties. Managing a family dwindles in importance next to the maintenance of emotional ties between marriage partners. And indeed the trend is reflected in recent law reforms. In the past, our laws held that marriage must continue as long as each spouse met his responsibilities. Now, emotional compatibility is virtually the sole issue. Our laws have not become indulgent; they merely reflect society's changing attitude to the nature of marriage.

Emotional bonds do not preclude self-realization. On the contrary, fulfillment is possible through such a union. The potential conflict arises rather between the *surrender* of one's self to another person and self-realization. Our vision has been blurred by Christian dogma which holds that one of man's (or rather woman's) greatest qualities is self-sacrifice. It is a woman's function to be the fertile ground for the spiritual growth of her mate—the power behind the throne. This ideal implies either that woman has no spirit of her own to cultivate or that she has a spirit but it must be killed off. It is difficult to assess which assumption is most outrageous.

10. See section on Dual Career Families.

We are dedicated to proving that two people can achieve the ultimate in self-actualization by refusing, at all costs, to surrender the self. *Make sacrifices—yes, but never human ones.*

Just as overlavish sacrifices can make for an unbalanced relationship, plagued with resentment, so can the seeming inability of many to throw off the desire to live up to traditional expectations. For example, men who write poetry or take up hairdressing are all too often judged to be "unmasculine." A woman who is not tempted to give up a satisfying career for motherhood is frowned upon as "unfeminine." Today, both sexes can perform most social functions equally well. The major exception—that of reproductive functions—is shortly to be dealt a severe blow. "The pill is like a popgun, compared to the howitzers and nuclear weaponry that lie ahead in the field of biology; the notion that babies can be raised outside the womb . . . [doesn't] lie 50 or 100 years in the future; if you talk to scientists working on this, you get estimates of ten years."[11]

Meanwhile, the persistent and rigid resistance to role diffusion is genuinely frustrating for those seeking self-expression outside the boundaries of traditionally defined sex roles. For centuries, man has been forced to adopt the role of physical aggressor while the woman remained at home to gestate, out of sheer necessity. Now for the first time he has a choice. What does he do? Elizabeth Jane Howard sums it up neatly: "For thousands of years, men have been expected to kill the mammoths which you cook" . . . now it is the man who goes "to the office to bring the pay check to buy canned or instant mammoth for the family."

If the prognosis looks depressing, take heart. The merging of roles does not mean that biological differences have been

11. Toffler, *Future Shock, op. cit.*

destroyed and that we are heading for a world of unisexuality. The people who *fill* those roles are still very much men and women.

What is clear, however, is that the current concept of marriage is anchored in anachronisms socially, legally and psychologically, and is therefore widely unworkable. Marriage is too often a disappointment. It is too often a relationship not relished but endured. And it is all too frequently a destroyer, rather than a generator of intimacy, perpetuated in order to meet the requirements of antiquated social expectations.

Before examining some of the various alternatives to traditional marriage that have emerged, let us see just what variations exist in our present-day institution of marriage.

Sociologists have unearthed the dramatic differences in people's expectations of marriage according to the social class from which they originate.[12] But apart from gross social class differences, there is tremendous variation within each social group.[13] One of the best researched studies of marriage was conducted by John F. Cuber and Peggy B. Harroff. Their book, *The Significant Americans*,[14] analyzes in depth the marriages of 437 American families where the husband had a highly successful career. Their findings must be alarming to anyone who hopes for human beings to gain stature and sustain growth through interpersonal relationships. They recognized five distinct patterns of upper-middle-class marriage.

12. See pp. 159–189.
13. Drusilla Beyfus in *The English Marriage,* Weidenfeld & Nicolson Ltd., London, 1968, provides a number of illuminating portraits of marital variation.
14. Published by Appleton-Century-Crofts, New York, 1965. Their five patterns of marriage were split into two groups: *Utilitarian,* consisting of devitalized, conflict-habituated, and passive-congenial; and *Intrinsic* marriages, consisting of vital and total relationships. We have simply changed their titles.

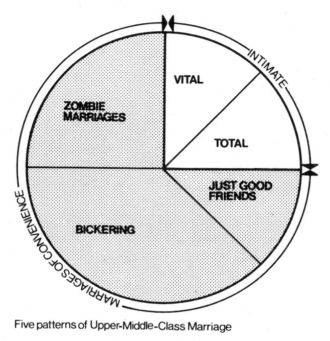

Five patterns of Upper-Middle-Class Marriage

MARRIAGES OF CONVENIENCE

Three-quarters of the marriages were of this type. This usually coincided with a high degree of success in the husband's career. The belief was prevalent that a successful career could only be obtained at the expense of an intimate marriage. Yet these marriages last. They are designed not to impede career success or to put other values ahead of it. Consequently, they are convenient and utilitarian.

1. Bickering

This is not an explosive relationship. It remains stable in spite of persistent nagging, arguing and bickering. The pattern of minor squabbles and petty insults are designed to keep any deep-lying conflict within bounds, for both husband and wife have too much at stake elsewhere to risk the disruption of divorce.

2. Zombie Marriage

This is an enduring marriage unlikely to break up even though the years have taken their toll of the warmth and intensity with which it began. As a couple they share few interests and talk little, and sex is routinized, if it exists at all. They feel despair and frustration, but they lack the motivation, courage and skills to enable them to revitalize their relationship or to end it.

3. Just Good Friends

This is similar to the zombie marriage except that it does not begin with any vitality. From the beginning it is amiable and functional, but it is not a close relationship. The prime value of the passive-congenial marriage is that it creates a placid and satisfactory home life with a minimum of inconvenience or personal involvement for people whose primary interests are elsewhere.

INTIMATE MARRIAGE

These are marriages that are valuable in themselves rather than because they support, and are subordinate to, career goals. These couples have intimate relationships, shared interests and an energetic degree of involvement in the marriage.

1. Vital

The most significant characteristic of a vital marriage is the exciting mutuality of feeling of its partners. Frigidity, impotence, menstrual problems and the like are rare among these couples. They are earnestly and sometimes fiercely monogamous. For most of them, outside relationships are either unnecessary or, even if appealing, too dangerous to the trusting and complete marital relationship.

2. *Total*

This is the mutual sharing of a vital marriage extended into practically every area of life—leisure, home life, career problems, day-by-day accomplishments and almost all thoughts and moods. People with total marriages may achieve worldly success, but they are likely to forgo promotions or appointments that might separate them from their partners or diminish their chance for interaction.

The Cubers found that although the intimate marriages approximated more the Hollywood ideal of the romantic relationship, these marriages were not necessarily more stable. As one brigadier general said:

> "You either have the whole splendid edifice or the damn thing tumbles down on you. There's just nothing halfway about this kind of life. . . . It is simply impossible to be insincere, living this way. . . . You're naked in this kind of mating."

The marriage of convenience is very stable because it is only likely to break up if it becomes unendurable. The intimate marriage is likely to break up merely if it loses some of its completeness and intensity.

Obviously each form of marriage reflects different expectations of what life should bring. But perhaps it is a pity that so few people manage to share the joys that can emanate from a growing changing relationship. However, it is important to remember that the total marriage is almost certainly a twentieth-century, Western, middle-class phenomenon.

In the past upper-middle-class men had almost always selected their wives on the basis of position, wealth, and sometimes beauty.

For companionship and intellectual communion they sought out other men's wives, and for sexual delight they sought out courtesans or mistresses. Only in modern life, and usually only in the upper-middle-class, has it become possible to find all these functions combined in one woman, so that a husband and wife may share friendship, sexual pleasure, romantic and tender love, parenthood, home life, recreation and intellectual or career concerns.

Morton Hunt

So much for some of the variations. But what are the real alternatives to legal marriage as we know it?

ALTERNATIVES TO LEGAL MARRIAGE

1. Trial Marriage

This is in no sense a new form of marriage or an alternative to marriage. It is merely a new means to the traditional end of legal monogamy. As a phenomenon, however, it has relevance to any examination of contemporary marriage. It allows for less painful and prolonged breakdown without necessarily lessening the feeling of commitment involved. And it may reflect a serious approach to legal marriage; otherwise there would be no point in experimenting with a trial marriage.

Judge Ben Lindsay, an extraordinarily progressive American judge in the 1920s, said, "If the trial marriage psychology puts too much emphasis on the risk, the psychology of traditional marriage bull-headedly ignores it altogether." Bertrand Russell felt that no two people should marry without first ensuring that they are sexually compatible. Judge Lindsay suggested a compromise such as "Companionate Marriage," which he defined as a legal marriage with legalized birth control, and with the right to divorce by mutual consent, for childless couples, usually without payment of alimony. In fact, the Romans practiced something similar—*affectione maritali,* a marital bond, not formally legalized, which could be terminated by either partner. Lindsay suggested that the easily breakable form of marriage should forbid children, while a second form of marriage, permitting children, should be virtually unbreakable. While this may never be adopted in law, society is drawing closer to paying lip service to the differences between childless marriages and marriages with children.

2. *Common Law Marriage*

Many people "live together" without any form of legalized commitment, either because marriage seems unnecessary or in an attempt to escape from the oppressive trappings of so-called security imputed to legal monogamy. But in no way are the relationships less permanent or less committed. For many, the notion of marriage may be as crushing as it is enhancing, and they feel that it should take its place alongside other institutions, such as the Church—that is, as a peripheral custom, essential for some and irrelevant for others.

An increasing number of young people are satisfied with "living together" until they contemplate children. This is simply because children are still potentially affected by the lack of a legal union, and will always be, as long as society places a stigma on illegitimacy. That children need security, emotional warmth and affection is in no doubt. But these qualities have nothing to do with marriage in the form of a legal commitment. They can only be the result of a spontaneous response, preferably in the context of an adult bond, based on caring and affection. The signing of a formal contract should not be necessary for a family unit to have security and social acceptability.

Bertrand Russell suggested that in a rational society marriage would only count once there were children. Sexual activity is a totally private affair and only has broader implications once it results in children. Based on the notion that children and not sexual intercourse are the purpose of marriage, proposals have been made for marriage to become annullable not just until intercourse has taken place but until the wife conceives. Until everyone makes rational and efficient decisions about contraception, however, there is a danger of recreating a form of shotgun marriage. Fertility may be adequate as the sole reason for marriage in Samoa but hardly justifies marriage in contemporary Western society.

One particular form of common law marriage is the "boyfriend" relationship, or extraresidential mating, in which the woman sets up home and the male partner is only allowed to live there as long as suits the woman. Hence she has power over granting privileges, which contrasts with the traditional marital relationship where the male has certain rights in the household and may even be the chief granter of privileges. There is no shared commitment to maintain a home; the partners simply drift apart when it is appropriate. In a situation where women are the dominant sex, some may find it amusing, if unliberated, to picture the male desperately pressuring the female into marriage! This form of domestic setup characterizes the West Indies, where it is not unusual for a mother to have four or five children each with a different father.

3. Marriage Based on a Renewable Contract
This suggestion bears witness to the fact that people change. What may have started as an extremely suitable match may after several years be rendered intolerable for the partners concerned if their needs have changed to such an extent that they are no longer compatible. Whether or not the match was suitable in the first place, it is hardly fair to punish people who have made one error of judgment at an early

stage in their lives by sentencing them to a lifetime of despair *à deux*.

It has been suggested that the renewable contract should be instantly dissoluble or renewable, after an arbitrary period of time, perhaps every three, five or seven years. This would certainly satisfy those who feel that the present legal system makes marriage too easy to enter into and too difficult to break out of.

4. *The Dual-Career Marriage*

The dual-career marriage differs from the "dual-worker" marriage in which the woman is expected to work only so long as her working hours fit in to suit her husband and children. Her work is considered less intrinsically important than her husband's, she is often only able to work part-time while family demands are at their maximum, and her income normally subsidizes vacations, clothing and other luxuries, rather than the family's bread and butter, which the husband still provides.

Dual-career wives, on the other hand, usually have a high degree of personal commitment to their jobs, while by no means negating the importance of family life. The authors of one study[15] of such families found that, while the combination of career and children provided major satisfactions, it also created heavy burdens, and couples almost invariably operated at a high level of strain. The major dimensions of stress were of five types:

a. "Role overloads"—both partners taking on too much physically and emotionally.
b. Dilemmas arising out of conflicting ideas about the roles of the sexes and reflected in the attitudes of friends, relatives and colleagues.

15. Rhona and Robert Rapoport, *Dual Career Families, op. cit.*

c. The maintenance of personal identity, husband and wives no longer having distinctive and separate roles, where the result may be competitive rivalries and difficulties in sexual relations.

d. The maintenance of the social network, where demands of extended kinship, friendship, and nuclear family responsibilities cannot be satisfactorily reconciled.

e. "Role-cycling" conflicts through a lack of "fit" between stages in the two career cycles and the stages of the family cycle.

The advantages of the setup are self-evident. Economic advantages are second to the opportunity the situation creates for self-expression and widespread satisfaction in a number of areas, simultaneously. In addition, the parents felt that their children were provided with a wider range of "role models" than is normally possible in a typical housewife-breadwinner setup.

5. Homosexual Marriage

The concept of homosexual marriage is not as strikingly new an innovation as may sometimes be believed. Among the Zuni Indians of North America, a homosexual could undergo certain rites, thereby rendering himself eligible for a recognized class called *berdache*. Thereafter he had the right to form a pair bond with another man.

Recent moves have taken place in the United States and Great Britain to provide some form of contractual agreement by which homosexuals can publicly state their commitment to one another. It is a strange situation in which none of the ordinary arguments for marriage are relevant. There is no social custom to which to pay lip service. There is so far no question of providing a secure background for children. And there is no morality to be appeased.

Many people ask themselves why two people cannot be content to share their lives, comfort and support each other and protect one another from loneliness, without the need for a formal contract. The notion that homosexual relationships are frequently as permanent and stable as this is, in itself, a revolutionary one for many heterosexuals. The stereotype paints a picture of one-night stands in public lavatories and "gay" bars. In reality, homosexual behavior is as varied and as potentially stable as heterosexual behavior.

Why should homosexuals marry? First, they want equal rights, which include the opportunity to marry. Apart from this, their situation is not so different from that of any childless couple wanting to marry. One might well ask the same of them. Catherine Storr puts her finger on the truth of the matter. People quite clearly do not want to marry simply to legitimize their children. In terms of their personal relationship, marriage provides a "framework for the future"—it provides a sense of continuity and permanence even if the legal document cannot guarantee these. Marriage is also a public declaration of that intention of permanence. If this applies to all couples who are in love, it follows that it is no less true of homosexual lovers.

6. Communes and Group Marriage

It is important to bear in mind that some alternatives to marriage are just that. They are not simply a new wrapper around the old product, a twist of the marriage kaleidoscope. Many advocates of the commune would be horrified to be labeled "married."

Commune life intends to be the answer to much of what stultifies and constrains monogamy—that "emotional gas chamber." It is an ideal directed against the family, seen to be the fount of all repression. "The community as family" represents the ultimate melting pot and maybe it *is* a viable concept for the future. But so long as it is not an acceptable alternative, it will take a good deal longer for communes to multiply on a widespread scale and establish some semblance of stability.

What then are the gripes of commune advocates? How have they set about devising a new system of intimate relationships?

First, their gripe is an economic one. The bourgeois trappings of marriage—the mortgaged house, three-piece suite and well-stocked deep freeze—the signs of security that so many women crave—are only relics of their feudal domination. The belief that security comes in the shape of personal possessions is a shaky one. But personal possessions in themselves are not destructive (even if they are a blind alley in the search for fulfillment) ; property only becomes dangerous when it invests people with the power to exploit others. And it is this that has led to the shared economy, the "collective consciousness" of the commune.

The role of women takes on a very different tone within the commune family. Betty Rollin, American women's liberation advocate, explains how the reaction to traditional female roles of housewife and housekeeper came about: "(1) room and board are not fair pay for housework and child-rearing, and (2) the only reason women are supported in the first place is that they have been brainwashed into thinking that's how things should be; (3) when women do get work they *still* have to be responsible for the house and their children (one study showed that husbands contribute an average of one to six hours a day of household work, whether or not their wives work. An English study found that working wives work an additional 5–8 hours per day in the home) ; (4) generally, women feel that whatever kind of work they may do, it isn't as important as their husbands'—the implication being that *they* are not as important as their husbands."

Some women are not talking about not fixing breakfast for their husbands so much as not getting husbands, not bearing children and not having a family.

Communes become a way to have a "family" without having a family. Feminists see nonsexist communes as ending female financial dependence on men and lessening the chores-of-living problems through sharing and distribution. They give their members the freedom to relate to a variety of individuals on an intimate basis, without necessarily acquiring spouse and children.

How do commune children cope with family life? Advocates reply that if two heads are better than one to think with, twelve heads must be better than two to love with. And it is hardly justifiable to attack communes for their instability, when traditional marriage is teetering on such shaky foundations.

Erich Segal, author of *Love Story,* says of the new-look family, whether it be a commune or a revamped form of monogamy, "The kind of family that doesn't differentiate between masculine and feminine but emphasizes only that which is human, that's a *great* thing. Kids will be enormously less hung up about sexual identity, their thought processes, about their life's values—because their parents are human beings, not Mothers and Fathers."

The aim is also sexual freedom for the woman so that she is released from the notion of man as her master and possessor. Communes differ in their regulation of sexual activity, but many of them advocate freedom from sexual restraint. This is not synonymous with rampant promiscuity, libidinous orgies and indiscriminate group sex. In fact, this very real change in sexual regulations may well lead to *less* rather than more sexual license.

The real innovation of commune life is a redirection of human values. Erich Segal sees the "large family, the tribe, as an obvious reaction to the dehumanization of the cities, against which the single family unit cannot compete." Commune life at its best attempts to satisfy the needs of intimacy, privacy and communalism. It aims to keep the positive values of the family—like the affectional side, which does not have to be based on blood ties—and to get rid of the negative aspects, like economic dependence and emotional suffocation.

In a *Daily Express* Harris Poll,[16] 94 percent of respondents thought the family unit was of crucial importance. Asked for their reasons, their replies were dominated by the following factors:

Need for a social unit/need to be close.
Support/help to fall back on.
Better to work together than be alone.
Security/security for children.
Guides/teaches children.
Family security means social security.

The significant aspect of those findings is that every point, without exception, applies equally well to commune values as to more traditionally based ones. The difference is one of

16. *Daily Express,* August 28, 1971.

definition and emphasis. For example, security is traditionally outlined in economic terms. The new emphasis is on emotional security within the context of personal freedom.

Research is still lacking in this area, but some of the first tentative findings suggested that many communes have foundered on bourgeois behavior structures—manifested in the form of status and power struggles, rivalries and petty jealousies. Many supporters, while not totally abandoning or belying their original ideals, have come to the conclusion that complete abolition of existing pair relationships is not realistic. It appears that pairing is almost unavoidable. Individuals find it difficult to invest an equal degree of unquestioning trust in several people at once. If this pair-bond tendency is innate, as some have suggested, it follows that the artificial suppression of strong spontaneous bonds may lead to deprivation. Some critics have gone as far as to claim that children for whom close relationships have been discouraged since birth may be rendered incapable of forming close bonds later in life. This and the resulting withdrawal are exactly what communes are seeking to avoid.

Intense one-to-one relationships encounter a special problem in the commune environment. A paired couple (whether mother and child or man and woman) is unlikely to attract support from its fellow members. The behavior of a paired couple conflicts with the all-pervading ideology of the group. It is at this stage of the dilemma that many couples have abandoned their commune family and sought support and satisfaction within either a "couples' commune" or some form of "group marriage."

One additional major disadvantage is shared by communes, group marriages and the extended family. They all restrict the freedom of the individual to move to where a job or particular life style attracts him. By definition, they require geographical, if not social, immobility. Where this was easily guaranteed for the extended family of the last century, present-day communes may find that geographical immobility does not fit well with the transient nature of their society.

THE EXPLODING MARRIAGE— DESTRUCTION OR RE-CREATION?

Marriage today is confusing and tomorrow may be almost unrecognizable. Our technical culture has severed us from our traditions. Our well-established expectations do not make sense in the context of the social upheaval around us.

Is marriage still possible to define? Is there any point in attempting to make generalizations about such enigma-ed variations? One hits upon a common thread and then remembers the multitude of exceptions. Perhaps one quality shared by all marital and equivalent relationships is that of commitment. The commitment may not be between the two marriage partners, A and B. It may be between A and C. C may be a political ideal, as in the case of a woman who marries a foreigner in order to adopt his nationality. Or it may be toward the mother who urges her child to marry a particular person. But hopefully, it is usually a more proactive one made by the people most closely involved with each other. The dictionary definition leaves no doubt about what this involves: "Commitment is an engagement that restricts freedom of action." Before those pledged to developing that freedom raise their hands in horror, it is worth pausing for a moment. It is clear that commitment does involve sacrifice, and if one is not prepared to go along with that the relationship is probably of little value. When reference is made to a person's "commitment" to marriage, what is being described is the degree to which that person is willing to compromise self-interest, personal ideals of perfection, indulgence of tastes, and so on, so that a particular relationship can continue. The alternative to making a commitment is not having a relationship at all, that is, remaining alone.

A committed relationship usually involves some degree of responsibility, even if this is self-imposed. It may be that the feeling of burden attached to many marriages is not actually the number of demands made by one's partner so much as the feeling that one partner is morally accountable for his spouse's emotional welfare. How much more demanding it is to live up to the expectations of the individual who has invested trust in one.

That responsibility, at its worst, can result in a devastating feeling of isolation in the nuclear family. Margaret Mead, the anthropologist, anticipates a move away from what we have come to think is the American family: "The post–World War II suburban family: totally isolated, desperately autonomous, unable to tolerate adolescent children at home, pushing its children out into matrimony as rapidly as possible, no grandparents, no cousins, no neighbors . . . with husband and wife expected to be all things to each other . . . this extraordinary overdomestication of men and isolation of women: this is what people think the American family is!"[17]

We are clinging to traditional assumptions in the face of fundamental change and now expect people to make it together for two generations instead of one—a rather astonishing bit of optimism.
Alvin Toffler[18]

Evidently we have two alternatives; there may be, as Toffler suggests, "a subtle but very significant shift to much more temporary marital arrangements." This would more closely match the radically increased rate of change in other aspects of society, such as change in jobs, neighborhoods, sexual patterns and leisure activities. And whether this be-

17. *Look* Magazine.
18. Toffler, *Future Shock, op. cit.*

comes a firmly established pattern or not, it is high time that we removed the premium on lifelong relationships, valued not for their quality but for their duration. People should not lose face if their relationships are less than permanent. We are not advocating the instantly disposable marriage, with its risk of emotional pollution to the environment. But it may sometimes be for the best if a marriage that is poisoning the partners is disposed of.

The other alternative is to accept temporary solutions and constant change *within* one enduring relationship. This is a far from easy goal to reach and marriage will probably become more rather than less difficult. But none of the alternatives so far proposed constitutes an all-embracing solution to the shortcomings of marriage. The essential thing is to keep searching out solutions. So long as a solution is being *worked on,* the problem is being managed. Resentments are aired, tentative answers are examined and compromises become possible.

A relationship in which there is growing intimacy rarely just happens. Rather, it is the continuing achievement that results from the self-investment of two persons who are determined to work at deepening the relationship—at turning the problems into possibilities. The art of intimacy, or relating in depth, like other artistic skills, must be cultivated through disciplined practice. Skill comes more easily for some than for others.
Charlotte H. and Howard J. Clinebell[19]

It is the *permanent* solution to any marital problem that is dangerous. It is inescapable and hence resentment toward it is liable to grow.

Resentment is more easily fostered in a marriage which

19. *The Intimate Marriage,* Harper & Row, New York, 1970.

depends on emotional intimacy. If a woman feels sourly toward a marriage based on traditional role expectations, she may feel able to turn a blind eye to the injustices by shrugging her shoulders and murmuring something about "men will be men." If, on the other hand, the marriage depends on continuing trust between the partners and a continuing belief in the other's commitment and understanding, the partners may not find persistence easy in the face of adversity. A relationship of this sort is vulnerable to disruption by any event which leads to loss of faith, or respect, or caring for the other.

What are we left with amid this holocaust of social change? An exploding concept of marriage, for one thing. But what remains is not just the fragments of shell. With any luck, we have started to chip away at the trappings that have ritualized marriage for too long, to reveal the kernel, the core, the *heart* of the matter, without the hypocrisy.

Postscript

This book is about change: social and personal change. This is the first time in our history that the span of an individual's life is greater than the length of time necessary for major social and political change to take place.

Marriage, be it legal or informal, can be a vehicle for change or decay, a trigger for excitement or mind-paralyzing despair, helping the development of your potential as a total person or castrating you into an emotional eunuch, perhaps still retaining the desires of yesterday but lacking the wherewithal to fulfill them today.

Becoming aware of aspects of yourself registers, in itself, that change has taken place. Total awareness means that you have control of your further development. Awareness, responsibility, growth—these are the elements of meaningful living. They are elements more realizable when working with other people than by analysis in isolation. How can you develop as a person using only your own fantasies as testing grounds? Life becomes a permanent dress rehearsal where the opening night never takes place. It is only through other people that we can truly come to know ourselves. This is why marriage, with its potential conditions of caring, trust and acceptance, can be the most important vehicle for developing a purposeful life.

How can you ensure that your marriage expands rather than deflates you? Try the following ground rules:

1. Live for the present. The past is a memory and the future debatable. Have dreams by all means, and enjoy nostalgia, but dream and reminisce because you enjoy it *now*, not because of what it once did or might have signified for you.
2. Learn to own up to all the feelings you have—whether pleasant or unpleasant. They belong to you. Don't deny them. They are telling you important things about yourself. Especially don't be afraid of passion—whether it be love or rage. Trust your feelings.
3. "To thine ownself be true." Acting phony only leads to phony relationships between images, not *real* people.
4. Do not try to solve one another's problems. Help one another to solve your own problems.
5. Learn to fight constructively.
6. Love without conditions, but never live together without conditions. No one can anyway, and it is better to discuss them openly than to assume that by some magic you both know what they are.
7. Above all, truly encounter one another as total persons with all your strengths and blemishes. In that way you can also learn to truly encounter yourself.

Searching for the ideal rose we don't see that each rose is the utmost perfection for itself. For fear of not finding the rose we seek, we hang on to the concept of "rose" and never learn that "a rose is a rose is a rose."

Claudio Naranjo

Suggestions for Further Reading

For those of you who wish to explore your human potential more fully within the context of your marriage, the following books contain exercises and discussions on various aspects of personal growth—these are the ones we have enjoyed and that have helped to develop our thinking.

Bach, G., and Wyden, P. *The Intimate Enemy*, Morrow, New York, 1969.

Blank, L., Gottsegen, G. B., and Gottsegen, M. G. (eds.). *Confrontation: Encounters in Self and Personal Awareness*, Macmillan, New York, 1971.

Clinebell, H. J., and Clinebell, C. H. *The Intimate Marriage*, Harper & Row, New York, 1970.

Downing, G. *The Massage Book*, Random House, New York, 1972.

Gunther, B. *Sense Relaxation*, Macmillan, New York, 1968.

Gunther, B. *What to Do Until the Messiah Comes*, Macmillan, New York, 1971.

Lederer, W. J., and Jackson, D. D. *The Mirages of Marriage*, W. W. Norton, New York, 1968.

Lewis, H. R., and Streitfeld, H. S. *Growth Games*, Bantam, New York, 1972.

Malamud, D. I., and Machover, S. *Toward Self-Understanding: Group Techniques in Self-Confrontation*, Charles C. Thomas, Springfield, Ill., 1965.

Otto, H. A. *Group Methods to Actualise Human Potential*, Holistic Press, Beverly Hills, Calif., 1970.

Otto, H. A. *More Joy in Your Marriage.* Hawthorn Books, New York, 1969.

Pfeiffer, J. W., and Jones, J. E. *A Handbook of Structural Experiences for Human Relations Training*, Parts I, II, & III, University Associates Press, 1970.

Prather, Hugh. *Notes to Myself*, Real People Press, Moab, Utah, 1970.

Schutz, W. C. *Joy: Expanding Human Awareness*, Grove Press, New York, 1967.

Spolin, Viola. *Improvisation for the Theater*, Northwestern University Press, Evanston, Ill., 1963.

Stevens, J. O. *Awareness: Exploring, Experimenting, Experiencing*, Real People Press, Moab, Utah, 1971.